Yield to Yield

Expanding the Kingdom of God Through Revelation of Your Destiny

Dr. Dan Lane

©2022 Dr. Dan Lane. All Rights Reserved.

Scripture quotations from The Authorized (King James) Version. Rights in the Authorized Version in the United Kingdom are vested in the Crown. Reproduced by permission of the Crown's patentee, Cambridge University Press.

Scripture quotations marked TPT are from The Passion Translation®. Copyright © 2017, 2018 by Passion & Fire Ministries, Inc. Used by permission. All rights reserved. ThePassionTranslation.com.

THE HOLY BIBLE, NEW INTERNATIONAL VERSION®, NIV® Copyright © 1973, 1978, 1984, 2011 by Biblica, Inc.™ Used by permission. All rights reserved worldwide.

Scripture quotations taken from the (NASB®) New American Standard Bible®, Copyright © 1960, 1971, 1977, 1995, 2020 by The Lockman Foundation. Used by permission. All rights reserved. www.lockman.org

The Christian Standard Bible. Copyright © 2017 by Holman Bible Publishers. Used by permission. Christian Standard Bible®, and CSB® are federally registered trademarks of Holman Bible Publishers, all rights reserved.

Printed in the United States of America. 1st Edition.

Contents

Foreword	v
Introduction	vii
1. Chapter One *The Kingdom of God and Man's Place in It*	1
2. Chapter Two *Spreading the Kingdom and The Fall of Man*	16
3. Chapter Three *Purpose Restored: Jesus' Ministry of Reconciliation*	34
4. Chapter Four *Manifestation of the Sons of God*	53
5. Chapter Five *The Priest Kings of God*	71
6. Chapter Six *God's Master Gardeners*	86
7. Chapter Seven *Shamar: Law of Unity*	107
8. Chapter Eight *Introduction to the Five Fields and The Field of Relationship of Our Body, Soul, and Spirit*	123
9. Chapter Nine *The Field of Our Relationship with God*	146
10. Chapter Ten *The Field of Our Relationship with Family*	166
11. Chapter Eleven *The Field of Our Relationship with the Church*	185
12. Chapter Twelve *The Field of Our Relationship with the World*	206
Acknowledgments	227
About the Author	229
Notes	231

Foreword

I first met Dr. Dan Lane in early 2002. He was driving my soon to be father in the Lord, Dr. Benny Charles Hand, to preach at my church in Darien, GA. It seemed a little odd to me that a man with a Doctorate was serving Dr. Hand in this manner, but I had not come to learn at that time about covenant fatherhood. As I watched how he served Dr. Hand for the last fifteen years of his life, I was able to observe what the Elijah/Elisha relationship was really like.

During those years I learned that Dr. Lane was more than a side-kick to Dr. Hand. I saw firsthand how God was preparing him to take the leadership of his church after Dr. Hand's death and move it into a new dimension. When that first meeting with Dr. Lane was over, I had no idea that he would one day become my spiritual father. However, at the time of Dr. Hand's death, it became clear to me that my new pastor had to be him.

While Dr. Lane is a very scholarly man, this book is written at a level that most Christians can understand. No one could do a better job of explaining covenant, five-fold government, and Christian relationships and duties than he does. Not only every Christian, but also every pastor can be encouraged by the deep insights of this book. "Yield to Yield" is a great book for developing disciples. While it is very scholarly, it is mostly about the discoveries Dr. Lane found while living out this timely book. You will better understand the nature of total commitment to God after reading this deeply spiritual book.

Lee Brandt, D.Min, Th.D., Ph.D
Pastor of Glory Worship Center in Darien, Georgia
Family and Marriage Therapist

INTRODUCTION

So, who do you say that Jesus is? Perhaps you are unsure, or your answer is that He is the Son of God and that He is your Savior. Now what? If He truly exists, then what does God expect of us? The answer is simple, but it is not easy. What have we experienced, or been taught, that the Christian faith is really all about? Is it all about joining a church and attending weekly services, praying over our meals, wearing Jesus Freak t-shirts, or trying our best to do good... or does God actually want more?

What does God really expect from us, including every person who claims to be a disciple of Jesus? How am I to live? What kind of relationship does He expect to have with us? Have we felt for a while that there must be more to Christianity that what we have experienced? Is there a purpose for us being born, and does God have anything to do with it? If He does, how can we know what His will is?

What God really expects from us is everything, the complete surrender of every area of our life! It involves much more than church attendance, more than prayer, more than tithing, more than belief in Him, and even more than self-sacrifice. God requires us to totally surrender our life to Him, a life of total commitment to Him and His usage. In fact, as we surrender more of life to Him, we become increasingly enabled as His co-laborers. As a result, He equips and empowers us to become world changers who actively expand the Kingdom of God throughout the earth.

I believe that we all can agree that our world is in dire need of change. The headlines of the news media are full of reports of pandemics, tyranny in governments, evil and wicked men preying upon the innocent, and the existence of a two-tiered system of justice. Then there are the wars and rumors of war as well as terrorism. The Adamic nature of man seems to be increasing in mankind as evidenced by the easy availability of whatever one desires to feed the lusts and appetites of the flesh. The earth is crying out for the manifestation of the sons of God!

Yield to Yield is a book of answers and actions that when applied, stand in direct opposition to the darkness in the world. This book also gives us the answers to what God expects of us. The author's purpose for writing Yield to Yield is to help raise up generations to return to mankind's original purpose for being created. We were destined to carry the Gospel of the Kingdom to the earth by making disciples of men and women, and by influencing the different systems of order in the world. We cannot complete our mission unless we impact both areas.

Our original purpose for being created was lost at the fall of man in the Garden of Eden. However, Jesus was sent to complete His ministry of reconciliation, which restored us back to our original purpose. Our purpose has been lost through the religiosity of the Western Church but is now being fully restored in this season. Yield to Yield is about restoring what was lost.

Yield to Yield instructs the reader of the different aspects of the original purpose of man. The reader will learn how to operate life in unity with our body, soul, and spirit; in unity with God's will and purpose; in unity with our family relationships; in unity with our church; and in unity with those in the world. This is not a book of dogma or of formulas, but rather a thirty-year compilation of Bible study, revelation, and life experience. Everything written in this book has successfully been utilized in real life circumstances and has resulted in the increase of the Kingdom of God.

It is the author's hope that the revelation in this book will be as much of a blessing to you as it has been to me. Please consider reading each chapter in the order written, and to memorize the challenge scripture at the end of the chapter. Then, seriously consider the "Questions to Ponder" section, and write down your answers to the questions in the "What God Says About You" section. Then, you will find that you will be able to act on the three steps in the "Becoming Who God Created You To Be", section.

As senior pastor of Fountain Gate Church in Auburn, Alabama and as President of Monteagle Institute of Theology, I have applied the principles and laws in this book in my own life. I have also taught other people these principles and laws, and as a result, they are successfully walking out their purpose for being born... all to the glory of God!

Dan Lane, D.Min., Th.D.

Chapter One
The Kingdom of God and Man's Place in It

> The world has yet to see what God will do with, and for, and through, and in, and by the man who is fully and wholly consecrated to him.[1]"
>
> — Henry Varley

So, what does Yield to Yield mean? Well, it starts with Jesus! We have all wondered at one time or another if our life has a purpose, or is life just random chance. Entire libraries have been written as men have attempted to answer these burning questions. Why are we here? Where did we come from? Where are we going?

Yield to Yield has everything to do with answering these questions of life. However, these answers start with another question. Who do you say that Jesus is in your life? If your answer falls short of Jesus being King of Kings and Lord of Lords, then you are missing something. In lieu of this, please consider this story.

> *Know ye not, that to whom ye yield yourselves servants to obey, his servants ye are to whom ye obey ... Likewise reckon ye also yourselves to be dead indeed unto sin, but alive unto God through Jesus Christ our Lord. Neither yield ye your members as instruments of unrighteousness unto sin: but yield yourselves unto God...*
>
> — ROMANS 6:16,11,13,19

There was a family who decided it was time for them to buy a home. After looking at multiple houses, they decided to purchase the perfect house. At the closing, the former owner came with the keys. There were 12 rooms in the house, but he was only prepared to give them the keys to six rooms. Surprised, the buyer said, "Where are the other keys?" He said," Oh you can't have them. There is a room on the second floor you can't have, as well as a room on the third floor. Also, there is a room on the fourth floor that I am sure you don't want. There's a dark place in the attic you can't have as well. Here are the keys for all the other rooms." Needless to say, they were very shocked at the owner's intent. Without any hesitation, they responded, "We want to purchase the whole house and want all the keys! If we can't have them all, we don't want any of them! It is everything or nothing at all."[2]

This illustration touches the very heart of what it means for us to be a Christian. Christianity is first and foremost a living relationship between the believer and the living God. It is not about a list of do's and don'ts. When we are born again, we enter into a covenant relationship with Jesus Christ Who desires to be a part of every area of our life. In the process of time, we discover that Jesus actually wants it all. This includes the warts, problems, issues and all the good stuff as well! He takes everything from cellar to attic: all the keys to our affections, all our hopes, all our ambitions, all our heart, all our life... or He will not take one key at all! It is up to each of us to decide. The best kept secret in the universe is that He gives us everything of Himself in return. We get the best part of the deal!

This story is so spot on, and totally ties in with the focus scripture for this chapter in Romans 6. This scripture refers to the use of, and the concept of the word, " yield". The word yield is used in two totally different ways in these scriptures. This is true in its usage in real life as well. First, in Romans 6:13b the King James version uses the phrase, " ...yield yourselves unto God". The word for yield is the Greek word PARISTEMI, which means to stand by one side; it means to provide a riding animal for someone to use; it means to assist or to place at someone's disposal for their personal use. God is conveying His heart to His children in this scripture. His heart is for every Christian to totally commit his life to Him, to put himself totally at God's disposal. His desire is for us to not hold back, or reserve, any part of our body, soul, or spirit from Him.[3]

In the Webster's dictionary this word means, to whomever you yield yourself as a slave, you are to obey. Metaphorically, it means to enter or to bring into one's fellowship or intimacy. Essentially the first meaning of the word yield, is to become His servant. This is a person who is intimately acquainted with the master that he serves.

What does this mean for us? Christianity is more than walking a church aisle, or of having a one-time salvation experience. Christianity is far more than the purchase of an eternal fire insurance policy that keeps us from going to hell. Upon deeper examination of the meaning of the word yield in this context, we realize that it means for us to make Him Lord and Master. He desires us to serve him. Indeed, the Bible is full of scriptures that teach that we are supposed to serve Him with all of our heart, mind, soul, and strength. Indeed, we are supposed to serve Him with everything in our life. Anything short of understanding Christianity in the context of His people making this type of full commitment to a relationship with Him, results in a false gospel.

The second meaning of the word yield, in Romans chapter 6:22, is that after we become servants of God, we are to bear or to yield a harvest of fruit. The nature of the fruit we yield is to be a reflection of His presence in our lives, of His holiness and of everlasting life. We are enabled by Him to bear this type of fruit in our character, thoughts, and actions. In the Webster's Dictionary, the second meaning of the word yield is to produce or to bear; to give in return; to produce, or to profit.

An excellent definition of the word fruit is given in the book, Sparkling Gems. "The word " fruit" is the Greek word KARPOS- the Greek word that describes the physical fruit of plants and trees. However, the word KARPOS is also used to depict the fruit borne by a person's life. This fruit might include a person's deeds, actions, moral character, and behavior, or the output of the person's work... Jesus used the word (to)... ultimately reveal what is inside that pearson."[4]

In John 15:16 we are exhorted to produce fruit that remains. The tense in the Greek language used in this verse means to continuously and to repeatedly bear fruit. This is very important for us to understand! The Bible teaches us that people will know us by the fruit we produce. To whomever we yield ourselves to, determines the fruit we yield. Our fruit can be of the Kingdom of God, as we determine to yield ourselves to Him, or of the Kingdom of darkness as we yield ourselves to our own selfishness and the lusts of the flesh. Therefore, we must determine to yield ourselves to Him in order to yield good fruit.

The Problem with the Western Church Today

Growing up in the 60s and 70s in the deep south Bible belt, I attended several mainline denominational churches during my formative years. Week after week, a common thread was preached from the pulpit. That is, man is a fallen creature under the influence of a powerful sin nature which separates us from a holy sinless God. The fall of man in the Garden of Eden created an emptiness inside each of us that can only be filled by His presence. There is only one way to have access to God and to have this emptiness filled through a salvation, born again experience. This results from believing by faith that Jesus Christ died for our sins, and that we can receive Him as our personal Savior.

The salvation message was delivered weekly in various forms in church meetings, often with the primary emphasis being placed on how bad and helpless each of us are. Our only answer and hope for this is a relationship with Jesus Christ. Please understand that this message is absolutely true! It is the author's intent to not devalue this message, which has resulted in multitudes being converted to Christianity. However, this is not the complete message of the Gospel of the Kingdom of God. We were taught to become a convert, but few were equipped and trained to become a disciple of Christ. This is a major difference!

I can use my own testimony as an example of this. First,

good fruit in my life occurred during my high school years when I accepted Jesus Christ as my Savior, asking him to come into my heart. In retrospect, this was the result of years of the sincere preaching of my pastors who had diligently sown the salvation message into my heart. Finally, the good seed of the Word of God had germinated and taken root in my life. Immediately, I became aware of His presence and of His peace and became a new creature in Him.

I knew Jesus as my Savior. But, I was totally oblivious to understanding His Lordship, as well as what to do with my life from His point of view and purposes. In the book, *The Hole in Our Gospel*[5] by Richard Searns, the author discusses this Lordless church dilemma. "More and more, our view of the gospel has been narrowed to a simple transaction: in marking a box on a bingo card at some prayer breakfast, in registering a decision for Christ, or in coming forward during an altar call. I have to admit that my own view of evangelism based on the Great Commission, amounted to just that for many years. It was about saving as many people from hell as possible for the next life. It minimized my concern for those same people in this life. It wasn't as important that they were poor or hungry or persecuted, or perhaps rich, greedy, and arrogant. We just had to get them to pray the sinner's prayer and then move on to the next potential convert. Our evangelistic efforts to make the good news accessible and simple to understand, we seemed to have boiled it down to a kind of fire insurance... There is a real problem with this limited view of the Kingdom of God."

Entrance into the Kingdom of God certainly includes receiving Jesus as our Savior. But, this also includes making Him the Lord or Master of our life. This lack of emphasis on the latter aspect of the gospel message can unintentionally lead to bad fruit being produced in one's life.

After being born again, I was continually exposed to the same evangelistic message in most services year in and year out. Meanwhile, the sin nature continued to rage in my members. I was given no teaching on how to live as a victorious overcomer in my life, or how to overcome the temptations that I was experiencing. I knew that there were scriptures that taught of a victorious, abundant Christian life in the Bible, but most of what was evident in my life, in my peers, and in their families, was essentially the same type of lifestyle that unbelievers live in the world. In other words, our lives looked just like the unsaved who do not know Jesus! Whenever I read the Bible, I began to realize that something was amiss. I knew in my heart that there had to be more to it than what I was experiencing.

Immediately after high school graduation, I moved from home to go to college and eventually quit going to church altogether. During those years, I was exposed to all manner of different belief systems. As a result, when I graduated I was a well-educated, spiritually confused Christian humanist. However, there remained a constant awareness in my heart that I was missing something. I now realize that Holy Spirit was gently pulling on my heart, drawing me to seek Him out. I remained in this spiritual state for ten years, living a life based upon my own desires, agendas and emotions. I was selfish and as a result, I was miserable.

At the age of 28, I finally met someone who had the answer to what I was missing. A coworker was living and walking out an abundant, joy-filled, and victorious Christian life. This elderly woman lived, breathed, and talked of a fresh and intimate relationship with Jesus Christ, Who was involved in every aspect of her life. This lady was hired by the company as an inside salesperson, and on her first day on the job she closed a big sale. This was unexpected since she was still in training and had limited product knowledge. Upon completing the transaction she walked by my desk and said, "That was totally God! He gave me that sale!" That got my attention! Over the course of the following months, she became a spiritual mother to me. The living witness of someone totally yielded as a servant of God not only impacted my life, but also the atmosphere of the business changed as well. Our store went from being the lowest producer in the chain, to being one of the top stores in a very short period of time. God blessed His servant's bold witness, and I found that the more I followed this godly matriarch's example the more I prospered as well. As a result, I began to learn how to submit my life to Him.

After wasting 10 years of my life living in a spiritual wilderness, I made the decision to receive Jesus Christ not only as my Savior, but also as the Lord of my life. I made the quality decision to sell myself totally out to pursue Him. I figured that He couldn't make a bigger mess of my life than it already was, so I decided to change my life by believing and living according to His word. I experienced an immediate change and no longer felt something was missing. I had finally found Him! This was merely the beginning of an eternity-based life of serving and of co-laboring with Father God in building His Kingdom. In the process of time, I have learned that there is a special purpose for my life which comes directly from God's heart. I also learned that the only way to accomplish this is by daily spending time at His feet serving Him.

In spite of my years at the university, I had continued to grow hungry for the things of God. I knew in my heart that there had to be more than what I was experiencing. Then, I found what I was looking for! I now realize that I was not alone in dealing with this issue. Author Brian Sanders discussed his observation of what many are experiencing in the book, Underground Church[6].

"In the end, we did not choose to leave behind traditional forms of church simply because we were frustrated... we were alive with the hope of the Kingdom of God at work in and through God's people. We were not seeing this hope in the churches we attended, even though we played by the rules. We were involved in everything... went to the services, attended the classes, and even taught the classes and led the services. But in the end we cannot escape the nagging, burning belief that there was more to the Church of Jesus Christ than what we were experiencing..."

The problem we have today in the Western church is serious; Another Jesus is being preached (see 2 Corinthians 11:4). Many are preaching and teaching a message of the Kingdom of God that consists exclusively of a Jesus who was sent by Father God to undergo an undeserved crucifixion, which subsequently led to forgiveness of sins. He paid the ultimate price for our redemption. This salvation message is absolutely true, however it is incomplete. This gospel message of salvation in Jesus Christ primarily brings about personal blessings and hope. However, it leaves out the critically important aspect of His Lordship. As a result, it does not fully deal with the solution to humanity's sufferings, frustrations, and troubles. The gospel of the Kingdom of God includes salvation through faith in Jesus Christ, but also it brings the Kingdom of God to planet earth in providing tangible spiritual and physical solutions to the problems of fallen man. This is all about God's original intent for us and why God has created us.

God's Answer in the First Principles

There is nothing new under the sun, and God knew the issues that we would face in our generation. He has already given us the answers in His Word... yield to yield.

Let's go back to the first principles of the Bible and consider the biblical narrative as given in Genesis 1:1. "In the beginning God created all the heavens and the earth." The Hebrew word used here for "God" is ELOHIM. The Hebrew word translated as "created", is BARA.

While sitting under the teaching of Dr. Ed Nelson, one of the most renowned Hebrew scholars of our generation, he provided me with these definitions which I believe you will find beneficial in your journey.

ELOHIM is used in plural form and means- rulers, judges, divine one, the (true) God. This word is used often for the kings of worldly kingdoms. However, when coupled with the Hebrew word BARA, which is singular, this exponentially separates God from all other kings. Remember, Moses received the revelation of the book of Genesis at Mount Sinai immediately after God had totally destroyed the ruling authority of the greatest king of the era, Pharoah. It was no contest! Biblically the word ELOHIM is used exclusively to refer to the Sovereign God who has created all the earth and all the heavens.His authority supersedes all others.But, His name also implies that he is literally a ruler over a Kingdom. His Kingdom clearly was in some type of existence even before creation itself came into being.

From the first four words of the Bible[7], we begin to see the important ramifications for understanding the concept of yielding ourselves in order to yield the fruit of the Kingdom. For better understanding, let's go a little deeper and consider the ancient Hebrew definition of the name ELOHIM. Please keep in mind that in the ancient Hebrew language each letter represents a number, a picture, and a letter. The pictures represented in the Hebrew letters of the word ELOHIM, is first, that of a yoke of oxen and the strength of that yoked team. The second picture in this word, is of a shepherd who has a staff in his hand which represents the authority of the shepherd over his flocks. When we bring these two pictures together we visualize a yoke of oxen going about doing the work that they are required to do, as they are being led by the shepherd.

The shepherd takes his staff, his authority, and leads the yoke of oxen in the proper direction and into the work they are to do. Great power for pulling loads, or plowing fields, is now available. The shepherd puts his light staff on his shoulder and connects it to the yoke on the oxen. He then leads them in the direction that he wants them to go in. The two picture graphs together represent the oxen in their yoke being led by the strong authority of the shepherd and his staff. They are led by an authority who is drawing them in the proper direction and into the work that the authority intends for them to do.

God's name of ELOHIM means the sovereign God, a King. Implied within that name is that there is someone who rules and everyone else is led by that Person. Can you truthfully say that you are faithfully following His Lordship in every area of your life? This is the heart of God for all of His children, and it is the only path available for us to reach our destiny.

The Kingdom of God

If ELOHIM is King, then He must have a kingdom. The Hebrew word used for Kingdom in the Bible[8], is the word MAMLAKAH. This word means dominion, rule, realm, reign, royal, or kingdom. The picture given in the Hebrew is that of a king reigning in a kingdom who is walking among His people. The covenant relationship established between the king and the people is accentuated. Combining the meaning of ELOHIM and MAMLAKAH, we begin to see a picture of God being a King who walks among His people. He gives them purpose and direction for their life. This is based upon the personal relationship between Him and His people.

Returning to the Genesis 1 narrative, we are taught that each of the six days of creation were good. This is true only because the God of creation is good. God is absolutely good with no darkness found anywhere in Him. Therefore, everything that comes forth from him is a reflection of this inherent goodness. Everything created, including man, was originally good because it reflected his absolutely good nature and character. As a part of His perfect and good plan, He placed man to live in the perfect environment on planet earth. Also, God delegated His authority to man to manage and to rule over it all.

In Genesis 1:26-28, our ability to properly rule and manage the earth is conditional. This is only possible through one thing, that God created us in His image and in His likeness. This state was required for us to have dominion. God's purpose in placing this requirement on man was to display His glory upon the earth for all to witness. This type of rule was not to be done through our personal power, strength, or will, but only through the power of God working in and through His servants. An illustration of God's original intent of this is displayed in the relationship between the earth and the sun. The moon puts out little light and energy of its own. However, it is the brightest of evening lights as it reflects the light of the sun. Man was made to reflect God's light as we rotate our lives around God. This is how we accomplish the purpose for our life.

The Hebrew word used in the scripture for image is TSELEM, which means to reflect God's life and His love. This word also gives a mental picture of, to be a shadow of, or to be made in the outline of something. The Hebrew word used in this scripture for likeness is the word DEMUTH, which means to be like something. We are to be like God in his behavior and in His attributes. We are to reflect God's compassion, graciousness, slowness to anger, loving kindness, and faithfulness. These attributes come from only one place, the presence of God. It is impossible for us to manufacture these character traits on our own volition.

Genesis 1:28 says,..." and God blessed them".... The word used for blessed is the Hebrew word BARAK, which means, a master and servant who come together to meet. The servant bows down to his master and the master in turn blesses his servant. The master tells him what to do and provides everything needed to accomplish his purpose. We will cover this Hebrew word in deeper detail of how this is used in our lives in a later chapter.

The entire process of taking paradise into planet earth is predicated upon His people willingly bowing before God as our King and Lord. This requires us to be disciplined in managing our time on a daily basis. Look for God to instruct us daily with all the directions we need. Not only will He give us direction, but He will also supply the tools, gifts, personnel, resources and money required to accomplish the purpose.

The true adventure of Christianity begins when we willingly bow our life down as a servant of God our Master. Only in the manifest presence of God will we receive His direction and provision. If we listen to Him with the heart to obey, we can expect to see His hand move as we co-labor together. Signs, wonders, miracles, and provision of finances and resources will supernaturally be provided. At times He moves in such a way that He will totally blow your mind. As a fringe benefit, He allows us to have the best seat in the house to observe and experience His power. But remember, He always gets the glory and the credit for everything that happens!

Daily as we seek His face in our personal devotional time, the likeness and the image of God will begin to manifest in us. This is not optional, but rather required to complete His purpose. The sovereign God sets the conditions on how His Kingdom is to work as well as how His Kingdom is to expand. As a part of this, God also sets the divine restraints on His servants. Our daily discipline of fellowship and intimacy with the King our Master is our source for power, authority, and ability required to do what God calls us to do.

MEMORY SCRIPTURE

And God said, Let us make man in our image, after our likeness: and let them have dominion over the fish of the sea, and over the fowl of the air, and over the cattle, and over all the earth, and over every creeping thing that creepeth upon the earth.-Genesis 1:26

QUESTIONS TO PONDER

1. Have you accepted Jesus Christ as your Savior?
2. Have you accepted Jesus Christ as your Lord?
3. If you answered yes to question one and/or two, is

there enough evidence in your life to convict you of being a Christian if you were taken to court?

WHAT GOD SAYS ABOUT YOU

Write your answers in a notebook.

1. Read Genesis 1-2- Write down everything about man's creation and his purpose in these chapters.
2. Read Ephesians 1- Write down everything God says about you in this chapter.
3. Read Romans 6:16-23- Are you free from the bondage of sin?

BECOMING WHO GOD CREATED YOU TO BE

1. Go to your pastor and request for someone to disciple you. Make yourself accountable to them.
2. Discuss your answers from the above section with them.
3. Make room in your daily schedule for a devotional time. Plan to read your Bible, pray, worship, and wait upon the Lord on a daily basis.

Chapter Two
Spreading the Kingdom and The Fall of Man

Every life should have a purpose to which it can give the energies of its mind and the enthusiasms of its heart. That life without a purpose will fall prey to the perverted ways waiting for the uncommitted life.[1]

— C. Neil Strait

"According as He has chosen us in Him before the foundation of the world... Having predestined us unto the adoption of children by Jesus Christ to Himself, ... being predestined according to the purpose of Him who works all things after the counsel of his own will..."

— Ephesians 1:3-5, 11 KJV

Life for most of us is a journey full of good intentions that often become shipwrecked from a lack of proper direction. Perhaps at times we have no idea of what we are supposed to do. For example, there are many people who graduate from college, get a job in their field, and then realize they are miserable with their job. By the age of thirty, they make a change and are in a field that they are really interested in. This pattern does not have to be true for a Christian. The Bible says that we can know the will of God for the direction of our life.

> And he said, The God of our fathers has chosen you, that you should know His will, and see that Just One, and should hear the voice of His mouth.
>
> — ACT 22:14

God is not a respecter of persons. If He did this for Paul, He will do it for us as well. God wants us to know His will and to know exactly what He wants us to do! This brings to mind an example of this spiritual truth which is revealed in the following story.

"It was the first day of football! I was in sixth grade on a team made up of students who attended school at Tenth Street Elementary. Our coach was an excellent teacher who had a heart for serving God, which was reflected in how he handled our team. He called everyone together, issued our equipment, and called us to huddle up. Then, he began to give instructions on exactly what he expected from each of us as he walked us through our triple option offense.

After a while, the team was split between the first team offense and the second team defense. Coach had the offense to huddle and the quarterback called out the play that we were going to run. We were all excited because finally we were going to be able to hit someone, and we wouldn't even get into trouble for it!

We ran the first play, and the coaches quickly stepped in to correct missed assignments. We huddled, and the same play was called. Again, as soon as the play was over the coaches stepped in and pointed out what everyone's assignment was and what mistakes had been made. As it turned out, we ran that play over and over that afternoon. By the end of the day, everyone knew exactly what Coach expected, and what each of our jobs were. As a result, most of us dreamed about the play that night!

As the second day of practice began, we huddled up to get the call for the first play from the quarterback. You guessed it! It was exactly the same play! We ran it and expected to have the coaches to step in and to correct us. However, this time it was different as everyone had properly accomplished their assignment! After running the same play several more times, a second play was then called. This second play of our triple option offense was very similar to the first play, except that the ball was handed to a different running back who ran to a different hole on the line of scrimmage. As expected, the coaches stopped us after each play in order to correct any mistakes that had been made, and to make sure everyone knew their assignment. For the rest of the practice, we alternated running those two plays.

Over the course of the first two weeks of practice, the coach continued to add options to the first play that we had learned. He added additional plays only when the team displayed that they understood their job for every play. When the first game of the season arrived, we had mastered six running play options which we could run perfectly, plus some passing plays as well. Coach had made sure that everyone knew exactly what he wanted and that everyone knew their job in doing it.

The Tenth Street Terrors went undefeated during that season. We also won a bowl game against a team made up of Allstars chosen from the other teams in the league. Many years later, I talked with one of the assistant coaches who had coached us. He told me that the school went on to win fifty two games in a row, including the seasons that I played. And, they still only ran those six plays!"

Today, I still think of Coach when I tend to be overwhelmed with the weightiness of the things I am called to do. It is easy to try to do too much! At these times, I remember to keep it simple and to do exactly what the Lord has told me to do. I'm not assigned to change the whole planet by myself. But, He has entrusted me with my portion and God holds me accountable to oversee it! It is up to us to seek Him, and He will show us exactly what to do.

It is the Father's heart for us to daily apply this truth in our lives. Let's consider how He created us and what our purpose is in establishing His Kingdom on the earth.

God's Purpose for Man

"In the beginning God created...". This phrase in Genesis 1:1 is truly a faith statement! We need to understand that the Bible does not contain one scripture that attempts to prove that ELOHIM exists. Therefore, we must be willing to trust what the Word says is true, accepting the consequences of this in faith. If God exists, and the evidence in the created order cries out that He must exist, then each of us must account for ELOHIM's reality and live our life accordingly. If God does not exist and the creation narrative of Genesis is merely a legend, then we can essentially live our life by our own set of rules and standards. This phrase in Genesis can then be personalized as, "In the beginning _____ (your name) created...". In essence, we make ourselves god.

Receiving the truth of ELOHIM's existence in faith is the prerequisite for being able to understand everything else that follows in the Bible. For example, in Genesis chapters 1 and 2 we discover that man was created in His image and likeness. Therefore, our existence is predicated upon the reality of ELOHIM's creative power. As we continue reading, the purpose of our man's creation is defined from this perspective. That is, that we were created to: willingly accept God as our Master; bow our knee in submission to our Lord; be equipped by God for our assigned task; take the glory of God to everyone on earth; and increase the Kingdom of God in spite of the resistance of enemies.

God has given us an important mission, which we accomplish as we serve Him and as we serve other people. All masters communicate their will to their servants, which necessitates a daily commitment of spending time with each other. This daily fellowship between God and His people is the desire of God's heart, and it results in the impartation of His likeness and image to each of us. This type of communication was displayed in the above story of the football coach who prepared his players by effectively communicating exactly what he wanted done.

Accomplishing our purpose is directly related to this truth. So then, how does this play out in the biblical narrative?

God blessed them...

— GENESIS
1:28

Remember the word, "blessed", is translated from the Hebrew word BARAK. But, why did God bless them? This verse gives the answer, "and told man to be fruitful, multiply, and replenish the earth." In other words, we are to go into all the earth to reproduce ourselves and to spread the Kingdom of God. Where have we seen this command before? In the following New Testament scripture, this same admonition is given by Jesus Christ to His disciples and is called the Great Commission.

Matthew 28:18-20 And Jesus came and spoke unto them, saying, All power is given unto Me in heaven and earth. Go you therefore, and teach all nations, baptizing them... Teaching them to observe all things whatsoever I have commanded you...

In this verse, Jesus confirms that our purpose is exactly the same today and has not changed from God's original intent. But, we must submit to Him as our Lord.

How important is it for us to submit to Him as our Lord? The word Lord, used for the name of God, is used 7900 times in the Bible. In contrast, the word Savior is only used 37 times. Did that get your attention? There is a much heavier emphasis in the Bible upon God becoming our Lord and Master, than in being our Savior. It is not even close. This does not line up with the current mantra in most Christian circles today. There is supposed to be a lot more to our relationship with Jesus than salvation alone!

Ignore this first principle, and we will never fully achieve our destiny. God's intention is to provide an abundant, joy-filled life for His children. But without understanding His Lordship, this will never be fully realized.

It is true that God created us with free will. But, He does not give us discretion as to how we are to take His likeness and image to planet earth. In His divine wisdom, God has specified three aspects of our life that we are to properly manage in order to spread His Kingdom into the natural world. The Bible defines each of these aspects as a type of seed.

INTRODUCTION OF THE THREE SEEDS OF THE KINGDOM

The Bible teaches that there are three types of seed that God gives us the responsibility to properly manage. These types of seed are not as a physical grain of corn, but are rather inner strongholds of thought, motivation, and character. These flow from the inner man and directly impact our actions, spoken words, and passion.

> *And God said, Let us make man in our image,*
> *after our likeness: and let them have*
> *dominion...*
>
> — GENESIS 1:26

In introducing the first type of seed, the seed of rule[2] deals with all issues pertaining to dominion: to authority, to ruling over, and to management of the earth. God has ordained that proper government exists in every situation and in every institution. Each of us is responsible for identifying authority in every situation. Sometimes God will delegate the authority to us, other times to other people. This is the seed of the heart.

> *Now the parable is this: The seed is the word of God.*
>
> — LUKE 8:11

> *A good man out of the good treasure of his heart brings forth that which is good; and an evil man out of the evil treasure of his heart brings forth that which is evil: for out of the abundance of the heart his mouth speaks.*
>
> — LUKE 6:45

Whatever, or whoever, we submit ourselves to becomes our master. The master we serve and worship is recognizable by the words we speak. Once we learn this, we will find that after spending five minutes or less in a conversation, we can tell who a person's master is. This revelation in one's words can just as easily apply to serving God as it can to serving selfishness, or riches, or power. Also, If we really want to know someone's master, we need look no further than their checkbook to see how their money is spent, or review their daily planner to see how they spend their time. This flows from the heart of a person, and is the most dominant of the three seeds. Without a doubt, it is impossible for us to properly manage the other types of seed without first being faithful with this aspect in our life.

> *God said unto them, Be fruitful, and multiply, and replenish the earth, ...*
>
> — GENESIS 1:28

The second type of seed[3] is about being fruitful and multiplying. It is all about reproducing mankind, having children, and spreading out to occupy the planet.

> *For all the land which you see, to you will I give it, and to your seed forever. And I will make your seed as the dust of the earth: so that if a man can number the dust of the earth, then shall your seed also be numbered.*
>
> — Genesis 13:15-16

Proper management of this seed requires us to become unselfish and to take a multi-generational approach to everything we do. This includes the foundational concept of the sanctity of human life and its direct relationship to the decision making and application of the laws of the culture. It is paramount that we realize our uniqueness in being created in God's likeness and image. No other created being can claim this. This seed management also includes the importance of the stability and order of a culture that results from the marriage covenant. This is the seed of the body.

> *And the LORD God took the man, and put him into the garden of Eden to dress it...*
>
> — Genesis 2:15

The third type of seed is introduced in the Bible in reference to man's job as caretaker of the Garden of Eden. Man was created to work, including expanding and protecting the Garden of Eden. The Hebrew word for, ..." dress it"... means[4], to work as a servant, to produce, or to create something. Man was created to work and produce within the confines of God's purpose and plans. This is the seed of production or increase.

The success or failure of fulfilling our purpose and destiny is directly related to properly managing these three seeds. This is now impossible to do by ourselves, but through Jesus' sacrifice all things are possible! However, our born again experience is only the beginning, as He requires us to willingly give up our own plans, ambitions, and goals, and then to take on His ambitions and goals for our lives. The result is that we live life His way, and Zoe life flows from our hearts outward to impact others with His love.

How is this supposed to work? How is this supposed to play out in our lives? Genesis 2:15 gives us the mental picture of " the how"[5].

Introduction to Keeping the Garden: *SHAMAR*

> *And the LORD God took the man and put him into the garden of Eden to dress it and to keep it.*
>
> — GENESIS 2:15

God created mankind and gave us a mission. He took Adam and Eve and put them in the Garden of Eden, which was created for them to settle in, to rest in, and to be established in for accomplishing their destiny. He set up divine restraints, or well-defined boundaries, by placing them in His chosen location in His perfect timing. God defined exactly what work His chosen people were to be do and how it was to be done. The Hebrew word[6] used for Eden is translated as, "a place of pleasure". Eden was paradise, a good place for man to be. The Hebrew word for Garden[7] is translated as, "an enclosed garden". Mankind now had the goods! This included everything man needed and was the perfect venue to accomplish what mankind was created to do.

In lieu of this, God directed Adam to, "keep", the Garden. This word translated, "keep", is the Hebrew word SHAMAR[8] and is a key to actively fulfilling God's purpose for our life. This word is extremely important and is used 440 times in the Bible (KJV).SHAMAR means: to hedge about, to guard, to protect, to attend to.

SHAMAR is a horticultural and a military term. This Hebrew word draws a mental picture of a gardener taking a parcel of land to clear it of all rocks, thistles, and thorns; to plow it; to cultivate it; to plant seed; to water it; to fertilize it; and to remove any weeds that may come up over time. Mankind's assignment is to continue this process until the plants bear good fruit for the harvest. Simultaneously, we are to continuously be circumspect and build a wall of protection against predators and enemies. We are to take a defensive military posture as watchman on the wall, closely overseeing the entire process from cultivation, to seed planting, and finally to reaping the harvest.

I recently witnessed a living example of SHAMAR as I watched a documentary about a tribe in Africa. Their huts were built on stilts well above the flat surface of a flood plain, and were connected to other huts by walkways. The land was very dry and dusty, for it had been many months since there had been any rain. However, the tribesmen began to till the ground as an act of faith and to plant rice seed in anticipation of the upcoming monsoon season. Also, these tribesmen began to collect stones that they arranged in carefully organized piles on the porches of their huts. This behavior seemed to be very odd. However, the use of these stones soon became apparent when the expected monsoon rains arrived, flooding the plain as the water rose nearly to the level of the huts. At this point, there was more than enough water for the rice to germinate and flourish. The plants soon began to grow above the surface of the water, bringing the appearance of a savannah to what had once been a dry wasteland. As the rice crop began to mature, predators moved into the area. The hippopotamus was well established in the river system and now could move freely in what was once dry land. They would come at night to graze upon the rice, but the tribesmen were diligent and carefully policed their crop to keep these predators from devouring the harvest. When a hippopotamus was sighted, the tribesmen armed themselves with slingshots and the previously collected stones. These projectiles were effective in startling and in scaring off the predator. As a result of their diligence and hard work, they were successful in harvesting a good crop of rice.

These tribesmen probably had never heard the Hebrew word SHAMAR. However, their survival depended on mastering this concept! It is just as vital to our spiritual and cultural survival as well.

The story of the tribesmen protecting their harvest is a good picture of God's original intent for Adam and Eve. Please keep in mind that the Garden of Eden was a very small area as compared to the rest of earth. Apparently, Satan and his followers had already fallen and had placed the earth in a state of chaos. Many Jewish scholars[9] think that this was a state of nothingness. However, ancient rabbinical teachers described this state as being more than just the opposite of the created state; it was an active malevolent force we can best term "chaos".

God's original intent is the same for us today. But now, there are millions of us alive and available for the work. The football story mentioned earlier in this chapter illustrates the truth that we must hear and obey His instructions in order to properly accomplish the job each of us has to do.

The Fall of Man at the Garden of Eden

2 Corinthians 11:3 But I fear, lest by any means, as the serpent beguiled Eve through his subtilty, so your minds should be corrupted from the simplicity that is in Christ.

In Genesis 3, we find the written account of the fall of man in the Garden of Eden. Adam and Eve were actively pursuing their purpose in tending to the garden as they endeavored to expand paradise into the surrounding area. They were daily receiving their marching orders as they spent time walking and talking with God in the cool of the day. Over the process of an undisclosed amount of time, there arose an enemy in opposition to their purpose.

Genesis 3:1,5 Now the serpent was more subtil than any beast of the field which the LORD God had made. And he said unto the woman, Yes, has God said, You shall not eat of every tree of the garden?... And the serpent said unto the woman, You shall not surely die: For God does know that in the day ye eat thereof, then your eyes shall be opened, and you shall be as gods, knowing good and evil.

In Genesis 3^{10}, the enemy comes to the Garden in the form of a serpent. The word serpent in Hebrew is NACHASH which means to: hiss, enchant, observe closely, murmur, lying, or deception. This serpent began to attack by acknowledging the truth that God had set apart one tree in the Garden for man to not eat of. This was true. God established the pattern that He always reserves some part of the harvest which is to be set aside for Himself. We are not to eat of that portion! If we do, then it is at our own peril. God was very gracious in giving mankind the seeds and the fruit from all the other plants to eat. However, God has always reserved His portion for Himself. This also applies to the management of each of the three seeds that He gives us to manage. The serpent's strategy was to attack each of these seeds, and he still does this today.

- In Genesis 2:15-17, the serpent took the words spoken by God, and then distorted them. Every form of deception begins with a distortion of truth. Remember, it is always more dangerous to believe a lie than to tell one, and believing this lie was devastating.
- This blatant attack by the serpent against God's Word was <u>strategically targeted to destroy man's call to stewardship over the seed of rule</u>. First, Adam disobeyed God by allowing an enemy into His garden. He had authority to stop this, but did not. Then, Adam and Eve decided to not listen to God, but rather to someone else for direction. In the process, they rejected God's authority.
- The serpent was going for the knockout blow with his first punch. He knew that once man was incapable of properly stewarding the seed of rule, that the other seeds would be corrupted as well. This was in direct rebellion to God's authority, and

the ability required to accomplish mankind's purpose was lost.
- In Genesis 3:6-7, Eve looked intently upon the fruit until it became her focus. She reasoned that it was good for food, it was pleasant to look at, and as a result, her heart's desire was placed on eating the fruit. This was a <u>direct attack against the seed of the body</u>[11]. According to rabbinical writings, this temptation had a sexual context as Eve was seduced and stirred by her body's desires, drives, and appetites.
- In Genesis 3:8-9, the serpent presented the fruit as being a means to make man wise. This was a <u>direct attack against the seed of production</u>. Adam and Eve both ate of that which God had set aside for Himself. Through their reasoning and the action which resulted from it, they chose a new master for all of mankind to serve. Instead of serving ELOHIM as King and Master, now they served themselves as they believed that they could trust their own senses as a source of truth. They could now be like God, and could be the final judge of right and wrong for themselves.

Adam and Eve chose to live by their animalistic instincts instead of the majestic nature of God. Humankind was now radically changed from their original state. Since mankind and creation were so intertwined, the state of creation was changed as well.

They were no longer clothed by the glory of God, which had come upon them from their daily fellowship with Him. Instead, shame entered their hearts for the first time. As husband and wife, there should have been nothing more natural than for them to be comfortable with their nudity with each other. That which had been created as perfection and as being good was distorted.

In Genesis 3:8-9, Adam and Eve heard the voice of the Lord as a wind blowing in the Garden, which was a common occurrence. This was the time and the place where they daily had BARAK communion with God. However, this day was different! Instead of seeking Him and looking forward to fellowshiping in His presence, they fled and hid themselves. Sin always causes man to run from the presence of God. Of course, God immediately noticed that Adam and Eve had run from Him. At this point, we observe an emerging pattern that every person ever born can relate to. When a person disobeys God they experience shame, and then they try to run and hide from Him.

Not only do sinners become fearful and flee from God's righteous judgment, but they eventually try to place the blame for their disobedience on someone else. Does this sound familiar? This is the fallen state each of us is born into. Due to the rebellion of our forefathers, humanity is a broken race and is not what we were created to be. Also, through rebellion the authority to rule the planet was turned over to Satan. As a result, it became impossible for any man to accomplish his purpose for being created on his own volition.

In Genesis 3:14-19, the narrative discusses the fruit of mankind's disobedience, which resulted in curses instead of the original blessings God had intended. A curse comes upon the seed of the body, the seed of rule, and the seed of production. The net result was that it became much harder for man to provide for his family and to manage the earth. However, there was good news. Through the loving kindness of God, He made provision for us to be reestablished to our original purpose.

God spoke that, "the seed of woman will be in enmity with the seed of the serpent", and that this would eventually overthrow Satan's takeover of God's world order. This would be accomplished by the seed of the woman, prophetically referring to Jesus Christ the Messiah. Jesus Christ was sent to earth for the purpose of bringing salvation and to restore man's relationship back with God. But also, He came in order to restore man's purpose in taking the Kingdom of God into the world. Everything that had been lost in the Garden of Eden was set to be restored.

MEMORY SCRIPTURE

Genesis 1:28 And God blessed them, and God said unto them, Be fruitful, and multiply, and replenish the earth, and subdue it: and have dominion over the fish of the sea, and over the fowl of the air, and over every living thing that moveth upon the earth.

QUESTIONS TO PONDER

1. Who do you serve as the master of your life? Whatever you think or talk about the most is likely your master.
2. Are you faithful to your spouse and committed to raising your children to serve God?
3. Are you a selfish taker in life, or do you serve and give to others in the way you live?

WHAT GOD SAYS ABOUT YOU

Write your answers in a notebook.

1. Read I Samuel 12:24; I Chronicles 28:9; Deuteronomy 13:4; Exodus 23:3-6- Who are you created to serve as your master?
2. Read Ecclesiastes 9:9; I Corinthians 6:18; Hebrews 13:4; Exodus 20:14,17- Who does God expect you to be faithful to?
3. Read 2 Corinthians 9:7; Galatians 5:7; John 12:26; Exodus 20:12,17- Am I supposed to be a giver or a taker according to God's will?

BECOMING WHO GOD CREATED YOU TO BE

1. Ask God to reveal to you any type of idolatry in your life. Repent and turn away from it.
2. Take note of the words that you speak. Whatever rules your heart will be revealed by what you speak.
3. Take an accounting of how you manage your money. If you regularly run out of money before the end of the month, you do not have a money problem, but rather a spiritual problem. Repent and seek financial counseling from your pastor or mentor.

Chapter Three
Purpose Restored: Jesus' Ministry of Reconciliation

"Brothers, repudiate and denounce... the idea that Christ reconciles God to the world. But, proclaim in all the tones that can melt the heart, that His great mission to the world was to reconcile humanity to Himself." [1]

— David Thomas

For the Son of Man is come to seek and to save that which was lost.

— Luke 19:10

Am I Synchronized to the Light?

The people which sat in darkness saw great light; and to them which sat in the region and shadow of death light is sprung up.

— Mathew 4:16

When Harriet and I were married, God blessed us with three unique and wonderful kids. We really had a blast with them during that season of our life. We decided to spend as much time together as a family as our schedules allowed, and one of the things we enjoyed the most was traveling to different places. As one would expect, my salary as an associate pastor of a small church and principal of a school was not conducive for a large amount of travel. So, I called a family meeting and the unanimous decision was made to begin to camp as much as possible, a decision which allowed us to travel more often at a more affordable cost. This led to many great times and adventures!

One such occasion was when we decided to go to the Smoky Mountain National Park and camp at the Elkmont campground. We were there the last week of June, which turned out to be great timing. After several days of rest, tubing, and hiking, we noticed a large amount of late afternoon traffic on the road that ran along the campground perimeter. I knew the area and realized that there was nothing there that normally would draw such a large crowd. Out of curiosity, I talked to a park ranger who said, "They all are going to see the fireflies." This surprised me! Everyone who grows up in Alabama has experienced the fun of going out at dusk to catch fireflies. They are everywhere and are not a big deal. So, we decided to participate in the firefly experience, whatever that might be.

That evening we drove a short distance to a parking area that was in the park. We carried flashlights and camp chairs, and a park ranger gave directions for where to sit and provided us with red filters to place over our flashlights. We walked several hundred yards up the trail and found the perfect place at the edge of a meadow, which gave us a clear line of sight of a large part of the mountain. At dusk as expected, the fireflies began to manifest, and they became more visible and numerous as the sky grew darker.

As it became completely dark, an amazing thing began to happen! The fireflies began to synchronize their lights with the other fireflies which were in close proximity. In a short matter of time, this was happening all over the mountain. The mountain appeared to be covered with synchronized Christmas lights, with line upon line of alternating and pulsating lights. It was as though the insects were putting on a choreographed lightshow, as the darkness was pierced by alternating lines of light as far as the eye could see. This was really amazing and cool to watch!

As it turned out, we were witnessing the firefly mating season. Amazingly, this type of synchronization only occurs in two places in the world, the other being in China. In God's Providence, He had led us to a place where we could visually experience the light piercing the darkness. This is a natural reflection of the spiritual truth of how Jesus Christ was sent as the light into darkness and desolation for all to see. When we are born again, we come alive in Jesus Christ from His death, burial and resurrection. When we begin to BARAK, His light begins to glow in us as well. The more we obey and become like Him, the more our light shines forth and is synchronized with His!

Exodus 34:7 Keeping mercy for thousands, forgiving iniquity and transgression and sin, and that will by no means clear *the guilty;* visiting the iniquity of the fathers upon the children, and upon the children's children, unto the third and to the fourth *generation.*

In the last chapter, we discussed that Adam and Eve had

been removed from the Garden of Eden. Cherubim with a flaming sword stood at the entrance of the garden for the purpose of protecting it and of showing the way back to the entrance. The sword is important, which is a picture of the Word of God and indicates to us that an entrance will be provided into the garden in the future. We know this as the Gospel of the Kingdom of God and that Jesus Christ is known as the Word.

In direct opposition to the hope given by Jesus, Satan and the fallen angels have brought darkness, despair, and hopelessness to the earth. As a result, we have been unable to accomplish our purpose, as mankind grows more wicked over time. The historical pattern of fallen man is a progressive degradation from generation to generation. From what I have observed through studying history, nations tend to grow more wicked over time, and the people sow enough wickedness that they in turn reap God's righteous judgment on their land.

The Downward Spiral of Fallen Man

We have already observed that mankind was radically changed as a direct result of rejecting God as Lord. As a result, our ability to manage the three seeds became influenced by temptation. For example, the seed of the body is influenced by the lust and appetites of the flesh. The seed of increase is influenced by greed. Meanwhile, the seed of rule is influenced by selfishness. Man's irresponsible decision to abandon God's authority led to our every action being dictated by bestial emotions and desires. In other words, the poor choices of Adam and Eve have resulted in humanity being cursed! Let's examine the historical downward trend of fallen mankind in more detail.

Violation of The Seed of Increase: Greed

First, let us consider the depravity of man in mismanagement of the seed of increase. The seed of increase is now influenced by greed! In the Genesis 4:1-12 narrative, we read of the first-generation children of Adam and Eve, the twins Cain and Abel. Cain was a farmer who raised produce. The original conditions on earth had been altered by the fall, making it very difficult to raise crops. Able, in contrast, worked in animal husbandry as a shepherd raising sheep.

Over the process of time, the harvest arrived. Apparently, these men understood the need to sacrifice to and to give thanks to God. He had blessed the work of their hands in bringing forth the harvest, just as He does for us today. In Genesis 4:3, the narrative says, "in the process of time", Cain brought his fruits and vegetables to place on the altar to sacrifice. The term, "in the process of time", indicates that the produce was not of the first, best, or choicest quality. But rather, Cain's sacrifice was made up of the leftovers, as Cain had apparently consumed the best of the harvest himself. It became obvious that he had greed in his heart.[2]

In contrast to Cain's offering, Able brought the very best of his herd to sacrifice. He understood that His source of blessings came from God and desired to show honor to whom honor was due. Even though the fall had taken place, the awareness that God exists was clearly visible to both men, even as it is to us today. In Romans 1:20, the creation itself is a strong testimony to every person of the existence of God, and therefore everyone is without excuse for not choosing to serve Him. We all must make the decision of whether or not we will sacrifice our best to Him!

As a result of Able's sacrifice of his first fruit offering, God was very pleased and blessed him. As you would expect, God was not pleased with Cain's offering. God confronted Cain about the condition of his heart. Instead of drawing Cain to a place of repentance, Cain grew angry and his countenance "fell" and no longer was his countenance lifted to the heavens toward God. Instead, he rebelled fully by focusing on the material world and his bestial nature. Afterward, Cain and Abel went to the field and began to talk about something, which the narrative does not reveal. However, Rabbi Daniel Lapin gives us insight into what the Jewish historians believe was discussed,

"The glaring questions are what did Cain[3] say to his brother in the field? How did Abel's response precipitate history's first homicide? Recorded (Jewish) tradition fills in the gap, stating that Cain realized that acquiring the entire world was twice as good as owning only half the world, indicated his intent of the older brother to seize everything. Abel rejected this idea, leading Cain to achieve his ends by killing his brother."

As a result of killing Able, Cain is cursed from tilling the land and the land would no longer bear forth a harvest for him. Cain would never realize his bestial desire of having the whole world for his own personal prize. God is a righteous and just God, and always renders proper justice commensurate with whatever the violation of His laws may be. We see this reflected in the curse that now falls upon Cain and his progeny.

In the process of time, God draws Adam and Eve back together and they have another child to replace Abel. Seth is born and grows up to be a man who seeks after God. His progeny follow after God as well, until the seventh generation. Meanwhile, Cain has gone his way and soon becomes the father of ungodly progeny. His children lived their lives as animals, according to their base instincts and their selfish desires. They had no fear of God!

Violation of the Seed of the Body: Unrestrained Sexual Immorality

The next violation of seed management, as listed in Genesis 6-9, deals with the wickedness that had reached its fullness by the seventh generation. In this narrative the sons of God, who are Seth's lineage, began to intermarry with Cain's descendants. The wickedness of man was great in the earth and every imagination of his heart and thoughts were continually evil. The Jewish historians believed that this referred to extreme sexual deviation. Even Seth's lineage had been tempted by this. The Jewish author Lauren Eichler Berkun explains,

"The Rabbinic midrash attempts to uncover the nature of corruption in Noah's generation. Rashi explains "corruption" as "sexual abomination and idolatry." Furthermore, citing a talmudic midrash, Rashi explains the verse "all flesh had corrupted its ways" (Genesis 6:12) as an indication that "even cattle, beasts and fowl did not consort with their own species." Finally, Rashi asserts that "wherever you find lewdness ... punishment of an indiscriminate character comes upon the world killing good and bad alike." In other words, when the ethics of sexual boundaries are broken, the floodgates of divine wrath are unleashed upon the world."

Even though we do not have great clarity in identifying this wickedness as mentioned in Genesis 6:4-5, we certainly see the type of judgment that occurred in the following chapters. The righteous judgment rendered indicates that egregious sexual sin was prevalent.

Apparently, nearly everyone[4] alive had succumbed to the

pervasive immorality of the day. Noah was the exception! We read in Genesis 6:8 that Noah found grace in the eyes of the Lord. This was much like the grace which was later given to Abraham's nephew, Lot. However, God's judgment for this type of sin is not restricted to a one-time event such as Sodom and Gomorrah. Historically, when nations grow and prosper there is normally a pattern of a strong nuclear family which brings stability to the culture. The Roman Empire is a good example of this. In the early years of the nation, the institution of marriage provided the stable foundation for the culture to prosper. However, over a period of time sexual immorality began to appear, and then sexual deviation became prevalent. In the latter stages of the empire, sexual perversion reached its climax as the empire began to disintegrate.

Noah was a faithful man standing alone in an evil and perverse generation. Noah knew the voice of God, and he obeyed when God told him to build the ark. Through his faithfulness, Noah saved his family and the animals. We see a pattern displayed of a man seeking God with the intent to listen and to obey. The man followed His directions explicitly from beginning to end, with the fruit of the Kingdom being born forth. Noah understood what BARAK and SHAMAR meant. As a result, God remembered Noah!

In spite of his faithfulness, Noah was still under the influence of the Adamic nature. As stated in Genesis 9, Noah became a farmer after the flood, and planted a vineyard of grapes. From his harvest in the vineyard, he was able to make wine and became drunk. Even though Noah had apparently kept himself sexually pure and had been set apart from the rest of his generation, his children had been exposed to extreme sexual perversion in the period prior to the flood. As a result, Noah's son Ham walked up on his dad when he was in the helpless stupor of a drunken state. Noah had removed his clothes and was naked.

> *And Ham, the father of Canaan, saw the nakedness of his father, and told his two brethren without.*
>
> — GENESIS 9:22

The rabbinical teachers[5] of the Torah teach that this Hebrew wording indicates that this was a homosexual or incestuous act of some sort. What Noah and his family had been delivered from, was still present in the bestial nature of those who survived the flood. The pattern of the fall in the Garden repeated itself: consumption of a fruit, followed by being beguiled (by drunkenness in this case), which in turn led to nakedness, which finally resulted in an immoral sexual act. As a result, a curse was placed on Ham's children starting with his son Canaan.

VIOLATION OF THE SEED OF RULE: IDOLATRY OF ALL SORTS AND THE DEVALUING OF HUMAN LIFE

The third example of violations of seed management concerns the seed of rule, which took place in the Genesis 10-11 tower of Babel narrative. The violation of this seed comes to full fruition three generations after Noah. His grandson is named Nimrod, which means "mighty hunter". In the Hebrew traditions, Nimrod was not just a hunter of animals, but also of men, who he sought out to rule over. Nimrod was not a public servant, but rather a tyrant in the way he lorded over the people he ruled.[6]

In Genesis 11:1, everyone spoke the same language and were able to communicate freely. Nimrod led the people to gather in one place to build a tower, as globalism was being birthed with the intent of making a huge tower the symbol of the new world order. His intent was to build a refuge to survive the impact of another flood, thus rejecting God's right for judgment of the sins of man. Nimrod shook his fist at God in rebellion!

Hebrew scholars also believe that the tower was directly related to occultic worship and practices. In other words, this tower marked the creation of a memorial recognizing the rejection of the worship of ELOHIM, and the establishment of the worship of false gods. Babylon, the city founded by Nimrod, was historically known for the atrocity of humans being sacrificed.

God's original intent was for us to spread across the planet and to increase the Kingdom of God. This plan did not include everyone gathering in a city and forming a one-world government. As a result, God came with His righteous judgment and confounded their language so that they could not communicate. Then, He scattered them across the earth. History is littered with the ebb and flow of great empires that arise and fall. There are those that appeared to be invincible as they broadened the reach of their borders and appeared to be well on their way to world conquest. Historically, these empires have always collapsed, and this will be true until Jesus comes back to claim His throne.

The truth is that we have a very clear choice each of us must make. Either we will love Jesus and serve Him, or we will love the world and serve Satan.

> *Love not the world, neither the things that are in the world. If any man love the world, the love of the Father is not in him. For all that is in the world, the lust of the flesh, and the lust of the eyes, and the pride of life, is not of the Father, but is of the world. And the world passes away, and the lust thereof: but he that does the will of God abides forever.*
>
> — 1 John 2:15-17

It is amazing that it only took a few generations from the fall in the Garden for man to fall to the bestial state of depravity that still exists on much of the earth to this day. The darkness is real, but is exactly where we are to take the light of God's Kingdom. It is time to consider what Jesus has done to make this possible.

The Temptation of Jesus: The Overcomer

> *The people which sat in darkness saw great light; and to them which sat in the region and shadow of death light is sprung up. From that time Jesus began to preach, and to say, Repent: for the kingdom of heaven is at hand.*
>
> — Matthew 4:16-17

The time had finally arrived for the fulfillment of the Genesis 3:15 prophetic word concerning the seed of woman coming to earth in order to defeat the seed of the serpent. Jesus was destined to bring light into the most desolate and darkest places. He was born to a virgin in a manger and as a result His name is Immanuel, God with us. Jesus Christ was crucified on the cross, and He sacrificed Himself to this type of death for us. He ascended on high and sent the Holy Spirit to come to live in us. Instead of the existing oppression and hopelessness of the fallen condition of man, hope has finally arrived. This hope lives today as He is with us, for us, and in us, which results in the good news that we have been restored to our purpose! Jesus paved the way!

In the beginning of the gospel narrative, Jesus went to the Jordan river to be baptized by John the Baptist. As soon as he rose from the water He was baptized in the Holy Spirit. Holy Spirit led Him to go out into the wilderness for 40 days and 40 nights, and as He became hungry the devil chose to tempt him. The devil is not creative, and he attacked Jesus in much the same way as he did Eve in the Garden. As always, the devil's goals were the same as he began his attack by trying to put doubt in Jesus' mind of what God had spoken. He always tries to put doubt in our minds about the truth of God's Word.

> *And the devil said unto him, If thou be the Son of God, command this stone that it be made bread. And Jesus answered him, saying, It is written, That man shall not live by bread alone, but by every word of God.*
>
> — LUKE 4:3-4

Each of the three attacks that the devil used are commonly used against all of us today. I have discovered that our response to his attack is directly related to how selfish and ambitious we are. We must evaluate our hearts as to whether or not we are trying to build our own empire, or are we trying to serve God and his Kingdom.

The attack by the devil is directly against the management of the three seeds. In the first temptation was an attack upon the seed of increase, or provision. Jesus had the ability to command the stones to turn to bread; however God wanted Him to live the same way as ordinary men do. In other words, Jesus had to decide if He was trusting God for provision, or did He trust Himself. Where will our provision come from? Will I depend on my own personal abilities, gifts, and talents, or will I be obedient and trust Him for my provision?

Jesus chose not to listen to the reasoning of the devil, and instead quoted the truth of God's Word as a weapon to stop the attack. In the process, Jesus gave us the proper example for defeating the devil by using this powerful weapon. God's Word is a devastatingly sharp sword, and when used in the proper way it destroys the works of the devil.

> *And the devil took him up into a high mountain, showed unto him all the kingdoms of the world in a moment of time. And the devil said unto him, All this power will I give you, and the glory of them: for that is delivered unto me; and to whomsoever I will I give it. If you therefore will worship me, all shall be yours. And Jesus answered and said unto him, Get behind me, Satan: for it is written, You shall worship the Lord your God, and Him only shall you serve.*

— Luke 4:5-8

The second temptation was a direct assault on the seed of rule. We all have the same choice of living a life to glorify God, or to try to make a name for ourselves. We have the choice of pursuing political power and worldly success, or we can choose to live a life of humility and of dying to self. We have the choice of lording over others, or of being the servant God has called us to be. There is no middle ground!

> *And he brought him to Jerusalem, and set him on a pinnacle of the temple, and said unto him, If you are the Son of God, cast thyself down from here: For it is written, He shall give his angels charge over you, to keep you: And in their hands they shall bear you up, lest at any time you dash your foot against a stone. And Jesus answering said unto him, It is said, You shall not tempt the Lord your God.*
>
> — Luke 4:9-12

In the third temptation, the devil gives Jesus a way to immediately gain a huge following. The temple was always surrounded by large crowds of people, and if they saw Him fall from the tower and caught in mid-air by angels before hitting the ground, the multitude would immediately follow Him. However, this would have compromised the truth. Jesus would have had to use the temple and Judaism to accomplish this end. The problem was, He was sent to destroy these things. The question we must all consider is, are we willing to compromise the truth in order to expedite purpose? Do we have faith in Him to promote us, or do we have faith in promoting ourselves through our own works?

> *And when the devil had ended all the temptation, he departed from him for a season.*
>
> — LUKE 4:13

Jesus overcame the attack of the devil. However, the tense used in the Greek in this scripture indicates that the devil eventually returns and repeatedly uses the same tactics. Through Jesus' (the second Adam) victory, the attack that led to the fall in the Garden of Eden, was overcome by One Who knew exactly what God actually said. Jesus passed the test as a man, and now is ready to begin His ministry of reconciliation.

THE MINISTRY OF RECONCILIATION

Colossians 5:17-20 Therefore if any man *be* in Christ, *he is* a new creature: old things are passed away; behold, all things are become new. And all things *are* of God, who has reconciled us to Himself by Jesus Christ, and has given to us the ministry of reconciliation; ... Now then we are ambassadors for Christ, as though God did beseech *you* by us: we pray *you* in Christ's stead, be you reconciled to God.

As soon as Jesus Christ had successfully[7] overcome the temptation in the wilderness, He began his earthly ministry. He first took the light of the Gospel into Galilee, the darkest of all the dark places. For generations, this region had been a hotbed of idolatry and demonic activity. Israel had split into two kingdoms, Judah, and the Northern Kingdom, at Solomon's death and Jeroboam became the first king of the northern Kingdom. One of the first things he did was to replace the worship of Jehovah with the worship of golden calf idols. These were placed in Dan in the north, and in Bethel in the south. The worship of these idols was soon more popular than the worship in the temple located in Jerusalem. As a result, the spiritual atmosphere became dark, hopeless, and oppressive. Anywhere there is idol worship, there is also demonic activity.

Jesus came to give hope to the hopeless and to set the captives[8] of darkness free. He was sent to establish the ministry of reconciliation for this purpose. Reconciliation is the Greek word KATTALLAGE, which is a compound word made up of the root word KATA, which refers to how one stands relative to another in time or space. The second Greek root word is ALLASSO, which means a change that occurs from one person toward another. When you put these two words together, you get the meaning of restoration of someone who is restored to a position of lost favor. In the context of what Jesus Christ came on earth to do, restoration means to restore someone to the divine purpose, or the restoration of a person to divine favor. This brings great clarity of His mission which was given for Jesus to accomplish. Through receiving in faith His work of atonement on the cross, we can now have a relationship with Jesus Christ and can be restored to the original purpose for being created as well. Hallelujah!

What was stolen by Satan is now returned, as the door to restoration has been opened. In 2 Corinthians 5:20, the word "reconciled" is the Greek word KATTALASSO which gives us a mental picture of God as the Reconciler in Christ. He desires to allow reconciliation to accomplish the intended results in each of us, for us to be reconciled back to God and our purpose. His desire is for us to change, and come into unity with Him.

There are great ramifications that this work of God brings to mankind. As we yield ourselves to Christ with all our heart, mind, soul and strength, each of us may now be blessed in such a way that allows us to be a blessing to other people. Those who are born again, now fully belong to Christ as Lord, instead of belonging to Satan. We are now able to approach the Master as we worship, study the Word, or wait upon Him as we seek to hear His voice and to see what He is doing. This empowers us to take His directions to plant, water, and cultivate the three seeds of the Kingdom. Listening to our Lord with the intent of acting upon His instructions, will result in the successfully yielding the fruit of the Kingdom. As a part of this process, we become transformed into his image and likeness.

As we daily fellowship with Him, we come in proximity to the lovingkindness of God. God's love enables and equips us with a weapon of mass destruction, which disarms the enemy and destroys all of his schemes. This is the only type of love capable of tearing down strongholds of darkness and uprooting the gates of hell. This type of love then heals and rebuilds lives of those oppressed by the devil. This type of love determines the fruit and the outcomes that we yield for the Kingdom of God.

MEMORY SCRIPTURE

Therefore if any man be in Christ, he is a new creature: old things are passed away; behold, all things are become new. And all things are of God, who hath reconciled us to himself by Jesus Christ, and hath given to us the ministry of reconciliation; -2 Corinthians 5:17-18

QUESTIONS TO PONDER

1. Are you selfish or self-giving?
2. Do you have problems with your thoughts concerning the lusts and appetites of the flesh?
3. Do you trust God? Do you trust that the Bible is true?

WHAT GOD SAYS ABOUT YOU

Write your answers in a notebook.

1. Read Romans 12:3- What does God say you should think about yourself?
2. Read 2 Corinthians 5:14-15- Who should you be serving with your life?
3. Read Mark 12:30-31- Who are you supposed to love? What standard does God expect you to use in measuring how much to love your neighbor?

BECOMING WHO GOD CREATED YOU TO BE:

1. Begin a daily Bible reading discipline. Set your goal

at reading at least three chapters a day. You may not have time everyday to read them all, but make it your business to at least read something in the Word. This is food for your soul!
2. Read Psalm 32:2-5- Make a daily habit of repenting of sin in your life. This includes making the decision to never do that sin again.
3. Read I John 2:15-17- Beware of loving the things of the world, and instead love God with all your heart, mind, soul, and strength and love people as yourself! Look for ways to actively do both of these today!

Chapter Four
Manifestation of the Sons of God

Almost every Christian knows better than to live at their present state of spiritual maturity. Our standard of comparison must be Jesus Christ. We are to become like Him.

— Anonymous

Recently, I was talking with a friend who had attended a class reunion for the first time in many years. Apparently, it was a good time of fellowship with old friends, but it had also become a great opportunity to witness Jesus Christ to everyone in the crowd.

My friend referred to one conversation he had with someone who is a Christian. Over the course of time, they began to talk about the problems in our culture that have arisen in recent years. My friend could not help but marvel as he repeatedly heard the same answer for dealing with each of the problems of our day. They said, "God is going to handle it." In other words, he implied that we did not have to worry or do anything but just trust God.

There was obviously a lack of understanding of the historical perspective of those who have spearheaded the founding of hospitals, orphanages, public schools, hospice, and organizations which care for the poor. The church has repeatedly stepped up in times of great turmoil and need. A distinct gap existed in their understanding of what God says He does, and what role believers are expected to play in dealing with what happens on the earth. I have observed that every promise given to us by God is conditional. If I do my part, He does His.

Becoming Who We Are

> *...Jesus ... said, It is finished: and he bowed his head, and gave up the ghost.*
>
> — John 19:30

As Jesus Christ hung on the cross, He said with His dying breath, "It is finished!" Then He gave up the ghost. This marked the faithful completion of the assignment Jesus was sent to earth to accomplish. But what was finished? John 3:8 says, "Jesus came to destroy the works of the devil"! His successful mission now enables us to do what we are called to do.

In lieu of Jesus' victory, we must now decide between two choices. First, we must learn and live life according to the purposes of God. Or second, we must live life according to the purposes of man, which is much easier. God's people are to seek Him and learn how to live His way.

The Bible teaches that the true sons and daughters of God have always been those who are led by His Spirit. This does not make everybody happy. There are those, even in the Church, who are always in opposition to this truth because they are comfortable with their sin. They desire to have their religion and their sin as well. They are counterfeits who have a religious spirit. In contrast, the manifest sons of God are ready to make their appearance on planet earth in the form of the remnant Church. But, what does the word manifestation mean?

> *For as many as are led by the Spirit of God, they are the sons of God. For I reckon that the sufferings of this present time* are *not worthy to be compared with the glory which shall be revealed in us. For the earnest expectation of the creature waits for the manifestation of the sons of God.*
>
> — ROMANS 8:14, 18-19

The word manifestation is from the Greek word APOKALUPSIS. The Greek scholar Rick Rayner[1] defines manifestation as,

"Something that has been veiled or hidden for a long time and then suddenly, almost instantaneously, becomes clear and visible to the mind and eye. It is like pulling the curtains out of the way so you can see. The scene was always there, but the curtains blocked your ability to see it. This is the moment you see beyond the curtain for the first time and observe what has been there all along, although it was not evident to you. That is what the Bible calls a revelation."

The Bible teaches that God has a purpose for you specifically to accomplish. But, it must be sought out!

> *Before I formed you in the belly I knew you; and before you came forth out of the womb I sanctified you, and I ordained you a prophet unto the nations.*
>
> — JEREMIAH 1:5

God is no respecter of persons. If He did this for Jeremiah, He did it for you. However, we must somehow deal with the hindrances that emerged from the fall in the garden of Eden. Jesus Christ is the way, truth and life. He has already paid the price of redemption to restore us back to what was lost, which is activated when we are saved. As we are born again, Holy Spirit takes up residence in our heart and begins the work of changing us from the inside out. The manifestation of the sons of God is this ongoing work as Jesus is increasingly revealed in us.

"But all I must do is pray a sinner's prayer and ask Jesus to come into my heart and I will be saved, right? That's it! Now I become a Christian and all is well!" Sorry, nothing is free.

God has placed divine restraints of place, time, and methodology on how we are to work with Him. This requires us to surrender ourselves completely to the Lord Jesus Christ and to separate ourselves from the things of the world. He has a plan and a set time, and we are not to try to accomplish it in our own strength or in our own timing. What happens if we believe we know His will, we get excited and zealous, and we try to do it on our own. The Bible gives us an example of someone who tried to do it in his own strength and timing.

In Exodus 1-2, we read that Moses was raised in the House of Pharaoh in Egypt. He was a Jew. He was supposed to be dead from the proclamation of a genocidal edict ordered by

Pharoah. The midwives were ordered to kill all newborn Jewish male children. But, through the grace of God, he was not only spared, but he was placed in Pharoah's household to be raised. Many years later, a situation arose in the narrative where he went to check on the condition of his Jewish brothers. In my opinion, Moses' actions implied that God had already revealed to him what he was born to do.

Moses discovered that the Jews were being heavily oppressed, and he came upon an Egyptian who was beating one of the Jewish slaves. Moses attacked the Egyptian and killed him, thinking that his people would recognize him as their deliverer. Perhaps they would rise up and follow him in rebellion against tyranny. He knew that he had the goods! However, he had not properly prepared and was trying to accomplish God's mission through his own strength in his own timing. As an Egyptian military leader, he had responded using wrath and violence. God never uses the wrath of man in accomplishing His purposes.

If Moses had been successful in freeing the slaves in his own abilities, God would not have received the glory. Also, there was an extremely low probability that Moses' training would suffice for the survival of the nation in the wilderness. There would have been no light taken into darkness. Instead of success, Moses was run out of town. No one recognized who, or what, Moses was, including himself.

According to the Exodus narrative, Moses escaped into the wilderness. Forty years passed, and Moses was changed through the trials and tribulations he passed through, as well as the teaching he received from a man of God, Jethro his father-in-law. Then, Moses had an encounter with the Presence of God. Moses' preparation was completed by spending time in God's presence, by listening to His voice, and by receiving provision from Him for the mission. When he finally returned to Egypt, Moses was fully prepared and equipped in the right timing to do it God's way. Moses had synchronized his life with God's plan, and as a result he became the vessel to carry the Light of God's Kingdom into the darkness. He was a forerunner of Christ and of the manifestation of the sons of God.

IDENTITY CRISIS TODAY

> *But when it pleased God, who separated me from my mother's womb, and called me by his grace, To reveal his Son in me, that I might preach him among the heathen; immediately I conferred not with flesh and blood.*
>
> — GALATIANS 1:15-16

Just like in the confusion Moses dealt with, there are many in the Church that have an identity crisis today. Many people know ABOUT Jesus, but they don't ACTUALLY KNOW him. Consider these personal questions:

- Do I really know Jesus?
- Is Christ really alive in me?
- Am I living in communion with Him?
- Is His power really activated in my life?

God's heart desire is to reveal himself to the Church in a personal and intimate way through salvation in Jesus Christ. As we seek His presence and wait upon Him, we are blessed with an intimate knowledge of who He is. Simultaneously, His presence changes us into who we really are, the manifestation of a son of God.

Decisions for Overcomers: A Question of Values

In order to become who I am as a vessel set apart for His light, I must honestly deal with the following questions:

- Am I willing to pay the price of becoming the manifestation of a son of God?
- Am I willing to pay the price required for revival and a world changing visitation of Holy Spirit?
- Am I willing to pay the price of giving up my schedule and time to spend in seeking God's face as I wait upon the Lord?
- Am I willing to pay the price of reproach and of losing my reputation for being on fire for God?
- Am I willing to pay the price of disruption to my comfort and lifestyle?
- Am I willing to pay the price of daily taking up my cross in repentance and consecration as I become more like Jesus?

Did you say yes to any, or all these questions? If so, please understand that there is only one path that leads to the price we must pay. This comes only through prayer and repentance. A childlike definition of prayer is to have a two-way communication between God and yourself. On the other hand, repentance means to turn away from one thing and to turn toward something else. This is simple, but not easy. It will cost you everything, but you gain all of Him and the Kingdom of God in return. So, let's consider how we actually begin to become the manifestation of a son of God.

The Six Meanings of BARAK in the Old Testament

We have previously discussed the basic meaning of the Hebrew word, BARAK which first appears in Genesis 1:28. Translated as, "blessed", this word means that I am to be God's servant as I listen to Him as my Master. Much like a waiter who waits on customers in a diner, I listen to what He speaks and desires, with every intention of meeting His needs. This is a yield-to-yield proposition. I give up my own will and replace it with His, which results in me being enabled to yield the fruit of the Kingdom.

However, there are deeper implications for our lives embedded within the meaning of this word, BARAK. It is clear from the scriptures that God wants us to draw near to Him and He expects us to ask for direction and wisdom. This includes those who are hungry for His Kingdom and for His fellowship. So, let's consider the full meaning of the Hebrew word BARAK in the Old Testament as it relates to our lives today.

Genesis 1:28 And God blessed them, and God said unto them, Be fruitful, and multiply, and replenish the earth, and subdue it: and have dominion over the fish of the sea, and over the fowl of the air, and over every living thing that moves upon the earth.

The Hebrew word used[2] for, " blessed", is BARAK, which according to the Ancient Hebrew Lexicon of the Bible has six meanings. First, this word means to bow the knee, for a slave to go to his master and to show honor where honor is due. It is recognition of someone of a lower station in life who humbles himself in the presence of someone of a higher station. This would commonly be used in master-slave relationships, as well as in a parent-child relationship. When used in this context, the master recognizes the honor shown and speaks to the slave giving purpose, direction, and resources required to accomplish the work.

The second meaning[3] of the word BARAK is, to salute. The origin and meaning of salute has a military connotation and nature. The origin for this word goes back to the Middle Ages, and the word described what two knights in full armor did when they approached each other. Often, they would not know who they were facing, so they would raise the face guard of their helmets in order to expose their face. In other words, they uncovered their identity to the other person. God expects us to be real with him as we come to fellowship. In turn, He is always real with us. As we fellowship with Him, He will begin to impart Himself into our lives and hearts. As a result, we begin to progressively have our identity in Him.

The third meaning of the word BARAK is, mouth to mouth. This is directly related to the ministry of Holy Spirit, or RUACH in Hebrew, which means breath or wind. In Genesis 2:7, God breathed into Adam's nostrils the breath of life and he became a living soul. The picture in Hebrew portrays God reaching down from heaven, picking Adam up by the head from being on all fours as an animal, and breathing life into his nostrils and mouth. Adam immediately stood upright with his head up and facing God. No longer was he instinctual as an animal is. He now had the breath of the majestic nature of God in his life. This is exactly what God does to us when we enter His presence, as He imparts His love and power to us. We are always changed as a result.

These first three meanings of BARAK, deal with the aspects of how God blesses us. All the action comes from Him to us. There is no known substitute for these on earth. However, as with all the promises of God, there are conditions established that we must meet in order to experience these blessings on our life. We must first draw near to him! Only then does He draw near to us!

We now find that the next three Hebrew meanings[4] of BARAK deal directly with equipping us for accomplishing our assignments. The fourth meaning of this word is that we are given the authority and ability to speak words of excellence, the authority and ability to speak forth life or death, and the authority and ability to speak blessings or curses. All blessings are nothing more than spoken prayer and the resulting activation of His answers. This results in thanksgiving as God's people bless God in return for what He has done. As a result, ever increasing joy manifests in the lives of His people.

The fifth meaning of the Hebrew word BARAK is to make peace. God makes peace with us through His Son. In turn, God calls us peacemakers as we are equipped to carry peace to earth. His people are to do this as his priest-kings through the foundation of prayer and worship. This describes our role as a paraclete or intercessor, which is the Hebrew word PAGA. Two of the definitions[5] of this word apply to our purposes here. First, we are equipped with authority and power to position ourselves between man and God, as we intercede and witness to make peace between them. Second, we are to position ourselves between man and the devil. In our role as a priest king, we are to intercede to bring on earth as it is in heaven and to destroy the works of the devil. This concept[6] of being a priest king will be covered in a later chapter.

The final meaning[7] of the word BARAK is, to cause to prosper. God prospers the faithfulness of his people as he blesses the works of our hands. We are supernaturally blessed to be given or to produce wealth in order to meet all of our needs. In addition to this He gives us a surplus to be used to bless others and to increase the Kingdom of God.

These last three meanings of the word BARAK enable God's people to be a blessing to the nations. This original intent was repeated in Genesis 12 when God gave the blessings of the Abraham covenant. These are still available to us today through Jesus Christ. He blesses us so that we can be a blessing to the nations. He blesses us so that we can speak and confess blessings on others. He blesses us so that we will represent him as His ambassadors on earth.

The New Testament Concept of BARAK

If any of you lack wisdom, let him ask of God, that giveth to all men liberally, and upbraids not; and it shall be given him. Draw nigh to God, and he will draw nigh to you...

— JAMES 1:5; 4:8

As quoted in this scripture in James 1:5; 4:8, God still desires for his people to come to Him to have fellowship and to answer questions. The Greek tense used indicates that He desires for us to fellowship with Him often, or any time that we need wisdom. Also, as indicated by the normal usage of this Greek word, He expects us to be firm and resolute in what we ask when we spend time with Him.

The phrase, "of God", comes from a Greek word[8] which gives a mental picture of a person who comes up next to someone else, drawing as close as possible. That is, someone who stands side-by-side with another and tarries in their presence for a while. God wants this type of relationship, and He desires for us to come spend time with Him. The moment we get side-by-side with God, He reveals everything we need to know and understand. This does not work or apply to those who rush into his presence. Those desiring a shallow or superficial relationship need not apply.

The Greek word interpreted, "ask", means that someone is to be very bold and insistent in drawing near to God to ask Him questions and for direction. Not only will He answer our questions, but God will also touch our hearts. His touch changes us! When we meet his conditions, then He gladly opens His hands and shows us every answer we need. This Greek word also indicates that He has obligated Himself to do this. This gives a similar picture as the Hebrew word BARAK.

*Joseph of Arimathaea, an honorable counselor,
which also waited for the kingdom of God,...*

— MARK 15:43

Joseph of Arimathea[9] was a member of the Sanhedrin in Jerusalem, who was a highly respected man in the community. He was also a follower of Jesus. The Greek word used for, "waited", is commonly used to describe someone's hope or expectation. Our western concept of waiting is usually used in describing a passive activity, but this usage does not refer to passively hanging around to see what will happen. Waiting indicates an active, earnest expectation accompanied by a high level of anticipation. Joseph was a man stirred by a deep hunger and longing to see the Kingdom of God. Spiritual hunger is always a prerequisite to receiving the Kingdom of God. Joseph had the goods!

God blesses each of His followers today through Jesus' sacrifice, so that others may be blessed as we lay down our lives in sacrifice. In order to do this, we are to take up our cross daily and to sit in His presence.

The Discipline of Waiting Upon the Lord

> *But they that wait upon the LORD shall renew their strength; they shall mount up with wings as eagles; they shall run, and not be weary; and they shall walk, and not faint.*
>
> — ISAIAH 40:31

In Isaiah 40:31, the Hebrew word used[10] for wait is, QAVAH, which is a verb meaning, to wait for, to look for, and to help. The root meaning is that of twisting or winding a strand of cord or rope, and it was commonly used to indicate one's dependence upon something that includes the resulting order around a future event. Whatever God has promised will ultimately come to pass. We will not be disappointed.

This word[11] gives a mental picture of a servant who is waiting on his master. This requires the servant to spend time with him and to linger in his presence. This also means that he is to come into unity with him as he and his master are bound together for a common cause. Also, the servant is to wait for whatever the master might say or give to him, waiting eagerly with expectation for what is about to happen. Finally, this means to have an anticipation in looking for an expected end or hope for the future.

When we wait upon the Lord, we should not go to Him with the sole focus on discovering the will of God. This indicates a wrong motivation in one's heart. This is based on a religious spirit which focuses on works that we think will make us accepted by Him. The correct way to wait on the Lord to focus on our relationship with Him. This type of focus includes knowing four things.

First, as we wait on the Lord, we need to understand who we are as a temple of God, and that He abides in us. Wherever we go, He goes. Second, we must realize that we must do something! We are to do whatever we know that we are to do, based upon what He has shown us to do. Our heart desire must be to glorify Him in everything we do. Finally, we must have a burning desire to have something, a personal relationship with God. We must have Him, and desire to draw near to wait for Him. We anticipate and expect His fellowship.

Practical Guidelines to Waiting on the Lord

> It is *the glory of God to conceal a thing: but the honor of kings* is *to search out a matter.*
>
> — PROVERBS 25:2

Waiting upon the Lord is a discipline which every Christian should strive to master. This requires time and effort. I write this with an understanding of the schedule demands that our culture places on each of us. Please be mindful that this is not optional, and that we must find a way to make time for this in our schedule. God's intention is to conceal His word and the desires of His heart to show only to those willing to search it out. For this reason, people who are lazy and easily offended usually don't make it in the Kingdom of God. The Word of God and His Presence are offensive to our flesh.

Please consider the following guidelines which I have learned and used for nearly 40 years, which have resulted in great blessings in my own life. Whenever you wait upon the Lord and seek God's face:

1. Do not expect a quick fix, but rather expect that what God does in you, and with you, will have lasting eternal results.
2. Set yourself apart from all distractions and activities. You might need to go into the woods or find a closet in the house. Wherever you go, make God your focus! It is best to consistently go to the same place each day.
3. Prepare to carry your Bible, notebook, and pen. Write down everything God speaks or shows you. This reference will come in handy.
4. Sit quietly, pray, praise and/or worship God in all His Majesty and glory. Be sensitive to the leading of Holy Spirit, and expect that His direction will vary from day to day. Don't put God in a box!
5. Seek Him, not His power or provision, understanding that seeking Him will result in Him giving us the power and provision we need.

6. Expect and invite the presence of Holy Spirit. When He manifests, embrace His presence. Yield yourself to Him, and you will be renewed and strengthened.
7. Listen carefully, and He will reveal things that He wants you to walk out. How does He speak? First, He speaks through the Bible. We need to consistently read and memorize scripture. Second, He speaks as we listen to words of prophecy. We will profit when we do so. Third, God will often speak to us by what we see and hear around us in nature. Fourth, God speaks as we listen quietly for His still small voice. Learn to enjoy His peace in the process. God will speak to us by placing thoughts or mental pictures in our mind. Fifth, God has been known to speak in an audible voice to His people. Finally, God may speak through dreams and visions
8. Beware of other voices that will hinder you. We must learn to discern all the voices that are in the world. The voice of the flesh is based on experience and often will condemn us. The voice of fear, which is based upon reason, will come to paralyze our faith. The voice of the devil is the accuser who tries to intimidate us. Then, there is the voice of faith based upon our trust in God. God's voice will always be confirmed by the Bible.
9. Always use your safety net. How can I be sure that I'm hearing the voice of God and his direction for the purpose of my life? Could it be a voice that is deceiving me? We must test the spirits behind every voice we hear. If a voice denies that

Jesus came in the flesh, it is not of God. Whatever God speaks will be consistent with the Bible.
Also, there should be the witness of peace in our hearts from the Holy Spirit. And finally, we should go to mature counsel that we trust for confirmation.

Be aware that some people believe that in this age we can no longer hear Him. However, there is nothing in the Bible that indicates this. On the contrary, God doesn't have much trouble speaking where He can be heard. After all, He was able to speak to an ungodly prophet through a donkey and to Cornelius who was not saved.

As we wait upon the Lord, we can expect changes that will take place in us and in our life. We must remember that we are made in His likeness and image, and that our relationship with him is as the sun which shines its light which is reflected by the moon. From spending time with Him, God always imparts a portion of His residue onto our life. As a result, we are enabled to bear the fruit of the Kingdom.

MEMORY SCRIPTURE

Isaiah 40:31 But they that wait upon the LORD shall renew their strength; they shall mount up with wings as eagles; they shall run, and not be weary; and they shall walk, and not faint.

QUESTIONS TO PONDER

1. Do you really believe God has a destiny for your life?

2. Can a person really know the will of God for their life?
3. Are you willing to pay the price to become a son/daughter of God?

WHAT GOD SAYS ABOUT YOU

Write your answers in a notebook.

1. Read Jeremiah 29:11; 2 Timothy 1:9 - God has good thoughts about you. Write down what these thoughts are and how these should make a difference in your life.
2. Read Acts 22:14; Ephesians 1:18-19; Ephesians 3:14-19- Write down what we can know about the will of God from these scriptures.
3. Read Romans 8:12-19- What should be your focus on how to live your life?

BECOMING WHO GOD CREATED YOU TO BE

1. Add to your daily discipline- Daily ask God what His plan and purpose is for your life today? Then listen with the intent to change your schedule as needed to do it!
2. Confess daily that you are actively becoming a manifestation of a son of God!
3. Confess daily that your life has a special purpose!

CHAPTER FIVE
THE PRIEST KINGS OF GOD

> "Our true identity is found when we stop being "who we are" and start being who we were created to be."
>
> — WATCHMAN NEE

When did it begin? When did I really start to understand what my life was all about? The answer was revealed when I decided to deal with the question of, "Who do you say Jesus is?" I was at a point in life where I was searching for something, that I knew there had to be more to life than what I was experiencing. As it turned out, I needed to get my life right with God!

Please understand that when you begin to deal with the things of God, you learn to expect the unexpected. This was true of the encounter that radically changed everything! On that fateful day, I was making my weekly service stops for my business accounts. Between stops, while driving down the road in my Volkswagen van, Holy Spirit's presence and conviction had been drawing me all day. Finally, I responded by crying out and giving Him everything in my life, committing myself to live my life according to whatever the Bible says. Holy Spirit flooded the van with a peace unlike anything I had ever experienced. That decision, on that day and at that time, was the beginning of an awesome adventure!

Prior to my encounter with Holy Spirit at 28 years old, I saw myself building a successful business and retiring as a millionaire by age 40, which in retrospect would have been very boring in comparison. However, there was a totally different plan God had determined for my life, and there were things created within me that were destined to become activated only when I made Jesus Christ my Master. Otherwise, I found that I was blind to them. However, I had an inkling of what was there from a Career Assessment Test I took in college. I tested high in areas which projected me to be successful as a farmer, a teacher, or a contractor. I rejected those out right as being an error on the test results. In my mind, there was no way I was going to do those things. Famous last words! I did have a desire to be self-employed in my own business, which was actually 4th or 5th in the order of projected occupations.

Over the course of time, I discovered that I was gifted with the ability to cultivate interior plants as well as raising vegetables in the garden. Yes, the ability to be a farmer was in me all along but that was not all. Two years after my encounter with Holy Spirit, the Lord told me to sell my plant leasing business. Someone had already approached me to buy the business, so I took a step of faith and sold the only source of income I had to support my wife, our newborn daughter, and myself. Then, my wife and I waited upon the Lord to see what our next assignment would be. Amazingly, my pastor came to us the next day and offered me the job of principal and teacher of a new Christian school. I accepted and did this for the next 10 years. What makes this remarkable is that I hated school when I was growing up, and I never saw myself as a teacher or principal. But it was who I was all along. I had forgotten what the Career Assessment Test had measured. God had already put the gifts and skills in me to start a school from scratch, to work with kids of all grade levels, and to properly administrate the program. I have the gray hairs to prove it!

THE PRIEST-KINGS OF THE KINGDOM: GOD'S MASTER GARDENERS

What does the Bible teach that is in each of us? What is the potential that we can realize? Will we allow the world to define who we are, or our relationship with Jesus that defines who we are? What does it mean today to be God's master gardeners who take the Garden and increase it to cover the earth?

> *And from Jesus Christ,* who is *the faithful witness,* and *the first begotten of the dead, and the prince of the kings of the earth. Unto him that loved us and washed us from our sins in his own blood, And hath made us kings and priests unto God and his Father; to him* be *glory and dominion for ever and ever. Amen.*
>
> — REVELATION 1:6-5

The New Testament teaches[1] that each of us are made kings and priests in Christ. The Greek word BASILEUS, translated king in this scripture, means a leader of people, a prince, the lord of the land or a king. This is reflected by the Greek word used for "Church", EKKLESIA, which means a legislative body possessing authority to rule over a geographic area. The Western Church has moved far away from this original intent. However, God created us to rule and to have dominion!

Not only are we to walk in authority and dominion, but we are to be the priests of God as well. The Greek word[2] for "priests", HIEREUS, is used to describe those who offer sacrifices and devote their lives fully to service of God alone. This word is also used to refer to Christians, those who are purified by the Blood and are in a covenant relationship with God.

Another word for covenant is marriage, which gives us a vivid picture of what covenant actually is. For example, a woman leaves her old life and family to marry her husband. She takes on a new name, which in the Jewish mindset is directly related to the character or nature of the individual. She enters a new relationship with a new authority, going from her father's house to her husband's house. In essence, she sacrifices her old identity in life and puts on a new identity. In the ancient Jewish culture and mindset, this was one of six major life events that were called, "being born again".

With these New Testament[3] definitions of a priest in mind, let's consider the Old Testament foundation of this concept. The Hebrew root word for priest is KOHAN which means to act as a priest, prince or chief. Also, the priest was one who mediated in a religious service. According to the Smiths Dictionary,

> "...the idea of the priest connects itself in all forms[4] with a consciousness of sin in man. Men feel intuitively that they have broken a law. The power above them is holier than they are and they dare not approach it. They crave for someone to intervene for them by offering up prayers, thanksgiving,

and sacrifices. He becomes their representative in the things pertaining to God, and also may become God's representative to man."

What do we learn from this? What is in me as a Christian that I may not have yet realized? Consider what we have learned so far from these definitions and make these your confession:

> *I am to be a ruler.*
> *I am to offer up sacrifices to God.*
> *I am to totally devote my life to serving Him.*
> *I am to be in covenant with God alone.*
> *I am to be a mediator between man and God.*
> *I am to be a mediator between God and man.*

Exodus 19:5-6 Now therefore, if ye will obey my voice indeed, and keep my covenant, then ye shall be a peculiar treasure unto me above all people: for all the earth *is* mine: And ye shall be unto me a kingdom of priests, and an holy nation...

Remember, God's original intent for Adam and Eve and their progeny was to serve in tending to and in spreading the Kingdom. They were God's original priests on earth. God is always the God of original intent, as demonstrated when He gave men another chance to be His priests at Mount Sinai. God's lovingkindness is amazing!

Exodus 20:18-21 And all the people saw the thundering, and the lightnings, and the noise of the trumpet, and the mountain smoking: and when the people saw *it*, they removed, and stood far off. And they said unto Moses, Speak thou with us, and we will hear: but let not God speak with us, lest we die. And Moses said unto the people, Fear not: for God is come to prove you, and that his fear may be before your faces, that ye sin not. And the people stood afar off, and Moses drew near unto the thick darkness where God *was*.

Have we seen this reaction to God's presence before? As God's presence began to manifest on the mountain, the children of Israel began to be in fear from their sin. Instead of drawing near to worship Him, they fled and hid themselves. Remember, Adam and Eve hid themselves at the Garden of Eden? Instead of drawing near to their Master and bowing their knee to serve Him, the people told Moses to go talk to God for them and to be their mediator. They said," Just tell us what He says and wants us to do!" They wanted a ruler and cared nothing about having a relationship with God.

Following the rules of a master are a lot easier than developing and maintaining a relationship. This is still realized in the "do's and don'ts mindset" of legalistic people in the Church today. Relationship is not their focus! However, the good news is that God did not abandon us and He made the way through salvation and covenant relationship with Jesus Christ.

God's Priest Kings: Separate and Distinct

Ye also, as lively stones, are built up a spiritual house, an holy priesthood, to offer up spiritual sacrifices, acceptable to God by Jesus Christ. But ye are a chosen generation, a royal priesthood, an holy nation, a peculiar people; that ye should shew forth the praises of him who hath called you out of darkness

> *into his marvelous light: Which in time past were* not a people, *but are* now the people of God: *which had not obtained mercy, but now have obtained mercy.*
>
> — 1 Peter 2:5, 9-10

What do we learn from this scripture? What is in me that I may not have realized yet?

1. I am chosen by God. This literally means I was chosen from among many others as His first choice.
2. I am born as royalty destined to rule.
3. I am to be holy and set apart from the world for God's purposes.
4. I am to be peculiar, or different from those who are in the world.
5. I am a person of purpose born to show forth His light and glory.

The potential for each of us changed when we were born again. Jesus Christ has made the way for us to enter back into covenant relationship with God as well as to manifest as the sons of God. This requires us to search out His word and His presence to discover the truth of who He says we actually are, and to allow Him to transform us into that person. We are His champions and overcomers, regardless of what anyone has spoken about us or what we have thought about ourselves. We need to realize that we are a special, hand-picked, royal, holy, set apart, peculiar, child of God who is born with a destiny!

Paul's Prayers: Revelation of Who We Are

The Apostle Paul dedicated a lot of his writings to the teaching and the testimony of believers who are destined to become empowered in Christ to be sons of God. In the Book of Ephesians, two of Paul's prayers are recorded where he prayed that we would begin to understand the reality of this truth.

Ephesians 1:16-17 *I cease not to give thanks for you, making mention of you in my prayers; That the God of our Lord Jesus Christ, the Father of glory, may give unto you the spirit of wisdom and revelation in the knowledge of him.*

Paul had an understanding that a person would not be able to accomplish his purpose unless God revealed it to him. Paul's prayer was focused on Holy Spirit's role in enabling us to change, and how our understanding of ourselves is to change as a result.

From this scripture, we learn that God has a perfect time in which He wishes to impart revelation to us. But what was the revelation that Paul was praying for specifically? He prayed for God to reveal five things that we all need to realize and understand to become who we are. If we get our identification in these five truths, everything else will take care of itself as we hearken and obey!

> *The eyes of your understanding being enlightened; that ye may know what is the hope of his calling, and what the riches of the glory of his inheritance in the saints, And what is the exceeding greatness of his power to usward who believe, according to the working of his mighty power...*

— Ephesians 1:18-19

> *That he would grant you, according to the riches of his glory, to be strengthened with might by his Spirit in the inner man; That Christ may dwell in your hearts by faith; that ye, being rooted and grounded in love...*

— Ephesians 3:16-17

The first revelation[5] that Paul prayed for us to receive was for us to know what the hope of His calling is. The Greek word used for, "hope", refers to everything which deals with the future destiny that He has for our life. This destiny must be sought out by daily seeking His face, and it is literally the reason we were born. We have a future in spite of what any person or news media might say!

The second revelation[6] that Paul prayed for us to receive was for us to know how valuable we are whenever God looks at or thinks about us. God sees His image and likeness on each of us through the blood covering of Jesus. He looks at us and literally sees Jesus. When He looks at us, He sees one of His own family, His bride, and a co-laborer who is His friend. When He looks at us, He sees the glorious riches of our inheritance of eternal life. There is no reason from God's perspective that we should be running and hiding from him ever again if we are born again.

The third revelation[7] that Paul prayed for us to receive, is that we understand the great power that is within us from the indwelling of Holy Spirit. We are the temple of God where Holy Spirit dwells and abides. Therefore, every aspect of resurrection power resides in us to bring forth signs, wonders, and miracles, for the purpose of accompanying us as we testify that Jesus is Lord and Savior.

In John 14, Jesus told His disciples that he would soon be leaving them but would be sending them another Comforter Who was to take His place. Jesus was speaking of His upcoming death, burial, and resurrection. Shortly thereafter He would ascend to heaven to sit at the right hand of Father God. He was referring to the Holy Spirit who would come to abide with, and in, His disciples. When we speak of being in Christ, we are also referring to the indwelling presence of Holy Spirt. The Father, Son and Holy Spirit are one Person.

Fourth, Paul prayed for the revelation that God's presence is the only place that one's spiritual walk can be strengthened. God has ordained us to be more than conquerors over sin and darkness in our own life, and as a result, overcoming the trials, tribulations, and darkness in the systems of the world. Remember, the arm of the flesh has never been able to accomplish the will of God. If it had, then we would take the glory. We must never forget that God is to always receive the glory for what He is doing, and as we walk, that in His power we are to always glory and thank Him for what He does.[8]

Finally, Paul prayed for us to understand the necessity of building our life on the foundation of the love of God. I have discovered that in His presence is a spiritual river which exists within the hearts of born again people. When we learn to tap into it, the lovingkindness of God will flow through us to impact everyone we encounter. This love is a weapon of mass destruction to the darkness. Watchman Nee[9] had an understanding of this as he wrote, "My deepest awareness of myself is that I am deeply loved by Jesus Christ, and I have done nothing to earn it or deserve it. Define yourself radically as one beloved by God. This is the true self. Every other identity is illusion."

In summarizing the two prayers of Paul, one sees that he focused upon the revelation of God's hope or future destiny He has for us, the precious value our life has in His eyes, the enabling resurrection power that resides in us, the source of our strength, and the lovingkindness of God we are to live in. All of this is predicated upon our identification of living our life in Christ.

LIVING LIFE IN CHRIST

> *Which he wrought in Christ, when he raised him from the dead, and set* him *at his own right hand in the heavenly* places, *And has raised* us *up together, and made* us *sit together in heavenly* places *in Christ Jesus...*
>
> — EPHESIANS 1:20, 2:6

This scripture says we are wrought and sit in heavenly places, "in Christ". This union between us and Christ is not a superficial or peripheral thing. So then, what does it mean to live our life in someone else?

An example of this is what I observed when we initially began to build our Christian school program. I served as principal, athletic director and coach of our teams, and as well as commissioner of an athletic conference. Eventually, we had others who stepped up to help. As was often the case, I rarely had significant problems with the kids, but my dealings with the parents were a different matter.

Anytime you deal with someone else's kids, you can expect trouble! For example, I found that certain parents questioned every teaching, discipline, or coaching decision, as well as action taken in day-to-day situations that specifically involved their kids. Often, those parents were trying to relive their past achievements through their children. Those days had come and gone and were only memories of the past. On the other hand, there were those who were never successful in academics or athletics, but then saw a second chance to experience success through their kids. In other words, they were projecting themselves to live in their kids.

When we are born again, the Holy Spirit comes and makes His home in our heart. Over the course of time, He begins to change us so that we become more and more like Jesus. As a result, Jesus' victories become our victories. Jesus' thoughts become our thoughts. Jesus' assignment to take light into darkness becomes our assignment. This transformation empowered by Holy Spirit enables us to live in Christ.

The concept of being in Christ is at the very center of what it means to be born again. However, there is a problem with this concept in the Western Church today. In many of the churches I have attended over the years, one usually hears teaching about the Father, the Son, and the Bible. Rarely, if ever, do you hear teaching about the Father, the Son and the Holy Spirit. But, what does the Bible actually teach? This is an important distinction which deals with the core of the Gospel of the Kingdom. Without understanding who Holy Spirit is and what He does, we are left with a form of religion without the power of God. This results in another gospel being preached. The truth is that Jesus resides in us and we reside in Him through Holy Spirit.

John Murray[10] has written, "union with Christ is the

central truth of the whole doctrine of salvation". A.W. Pink wrote, " The expression being one with Christ is unknown in most professing Christian circles, and even where it is used it takes in only a fragment of this precious truth."

This is quite amazing when you read in the Pauline epistles the terms, "in Him", "in Christ", or, "in Jesus Christ", occur 164 times. This is significant and we do not need to miss this truth! James Montgomery Boice wrote,

" By use of these phrases, Paul teaches[11] that we are chosen " in him before the foundation of the world (Eph. 1:4), Called (I Cor.7:22), Made alive (Eph. 2:5), justified (Gal. 2:17), created for good works (Eph 2:10), sanctified (I Cor. 1:2), enriched with all speech and knowledge (I Cor. 1:5), and assured of resurrection (Romans. 6:5). In addition, there are several other scriptures that say in Christ, alone, we have redemption, eternal life, righteousness, wisdom, freedom from the law, and every spiritual blessing."

Please notice this is a comprehensive list of what it means to be a Christian. Without proper understanding of this concept, you will have another religion which leads to serving another Jesus.

In Ephesians, the scriptures clearly say that we are seated in heavenly places in Christ, which gives a picture in the Greek denoting a fixed position in one's condition or place. This does not mean that we are sitting in a physical chair over in a corner, but rather deals with how we define ourselves from the perspective of who we are in Him (John 15). We are no longer supposed to get our self-identification or self-worth from our job, hobbies, football team, family, etc., but rather from our relationship in Jesus Christ. His values are now our values, we think as He thinks, we feel the same way He feels, and we experience life through the lens of relationship with Him.

Galatians 2:20- "I have been crucified with Christ and I no longer live, but Christ lives in me. The life I now live in the body, I live by faith in the Son of God, who loved me and gave himself for me."

MEMORY SCRIPTURE

> *But ye are a chosen generation, a royal priesthood, an holy nation, a peculiar people; that ye should shew forth the praises of him who hath called you out of darkness into his marvelous light: Which in time past were not a people, but are now the people of God: which had not obtained mercy, but now have obtained mercy.*
>
> *— 1 Peter 2:9-10*

QUESTIONS TO PONDER

1. What is God's intent for the Church today?
2. What is the job description of a nation of priests?
3. What does it mean to be "in Christ?"

WHAT GOD SAYS ABOUT YOU

Write your answers in a notebook.

1. Read Ephesians 1:20-23; 2:6- Write down how these scriptures relate to the restoration of man's original purpose.

2. Read 1 Peter 2:5, 9-10- Write down how this describes you and your purpose.
3. Read Ephesians 1-3- write every way these scriptures indicate that we are in Christ.

BECOMING WHO GOD CREATED YOU TO BE

1. Add to your daily discipline- After God tells you your purpose for today, then determine to focus your faith for that day on the assignment He gives you.
2. Confess daily that you are chosen by God from among many others, handpicked for His service!
3. Separate yourself and your lifestyle from those who live in sin in the world.

Chapter Six
God's Master Gardeners

"God's kingdom realm is like someone spreading seed on the ground. He goes to bed and gets up, day after day, and the seed sprouts and grows tall, though he knows not how."

— Mark 4:26-27, The Passion Translation

Why did God place man in the Garden of Eden? He placed him there to do creative work! Mankind's assignment was to take the seed of the Garden of Eden and to create paradise on planet earth. This was to be in opposition to the influence of Satan's kingdom of darkness, nothingness, and chaos. Mankind was created to colabor with God to bring forth, "on earth as it is in heaven". We were made to create! Man stands alone in the created order of living creatures in that he was created in God's likeness and image. God creates! We are made like Him, and therefore, we have the ability to create as well! This means that we are able to take the raw resources of the earth and produce not only what we need, but to produce a surplus as well. We are created to help meet the needs of others and to build the Kingdom of God. God made men to be givers!

On the other hand, animals were made to live by instinct alone and were given the ability to create only through reproduction after their kind. God created nature to meet the needs of animals and, as a result, animals are able to flourish by instinct. There is no animal created to do what man does. Such is the world order created by God. Animals do not create and therefore are not givers by nature. Animals instinctually live as takers, focusing entirely upon meeting their personal needs. A person who is not born again also lives by instinct, having rejected God's nature, and he is a taker as a result.

Rabbi Daniel Lapin wrote[1] this insight concerning man's creative ability,

> "God placed man into the garden of Eden to work it,... this work was to be man's source of satisfaction. In this, he would fulfill his destiny as a partner of his Creator in the act of creation. Through work, he would prove that he was indeed created in God's image because he was to be earth's only creature capable of the same creativity as God Himself."

Indeed, mankind can take the raw materials available on earth and create what he needs. We do this through God's delegated authority primarily by the proper stewardship and management of:

1. The seed of rule- which is directly related to authority, rule, and worship. This is reflected by the words we speak, which will either be of life or of death.
2. The seed of the body- which is directly related to procreation, to continuance of the human race, and to the value of all types of life.
3. The seed of increase- which deals with how we create wealth and manage resources used to meet our needs and the needs of others. This includes financing the growth of the Kingdom of God.

Let's consider this in the following example of the seed of increase. Please note, tithing is a part of managing this particular type of seed.

One of the great joys I have had is to disciple young men. There was a time whenI had the opportunity to disciple a particular young man for several months and had begun to see growth and encouraging changes in his life. As a new convert, he had never been to church before and was essentially a blank slate when it came to the things of God. One day, he walked into my office and immediately said, " It doesn't work; I've tried it for two weeks and it just does not work." I had no idea what he was talking about, and he read my questioning expression. He then said, " This tithe thing doesn't work. I have been tithing for two whole weeks and I have not seen any change in my finances yet. It doesn't work." His response had surprised me, but then I realized that he was part of the fast food generation who had been taught to have everything immediately and to have it their way. He was still very much under control of the Adamic nature and was driven to be a taker instead of being a giver.

Does tithing really work? Sure! There is a universal law commonly called the Law of Sowing and Reaping, which always works whether we realize it or not. Just as gravity is always working, we can use it for our benefit or ignore it to our detriment. This is true of sowing and reaping as well. Money is only one type of seed which we sow and the sowing of financial seed in the form of our tithes and offerings is an act of worship to God. This is a matter of the heart, and has everything to do with living a lifestyle of giving as we express our worship and thanksgiving for what God has done for us.

In Galatians 6:7-8 Paul says, "Be not deceived; God is not mocked: for whatever a man sows, that shall he also reap. For he that sows to his flesh shall of the flesh reap corruption; but he that sows to the Spirit shall of the Spirit reap life everlasting."

The author Rick Renner wrote[2] of this concept of sowing and reaping and the necessary discipline which is required:

> "This principle is so true that Paul begins by telling us not to question its validity... the word deceived means to lead astray, to be led off course, or to be affected but an outside influence. This is the Greek word PLANAO, which depicts the activity of false teachers. Essentially, Paul is saying stop being deceived! ...It does not take but one word of doubt there, and some here, for a new believer to let go of their grip on their promises and walk away... Paul boldly declares what he believes that whatever you sow you will reap...The Greek word translated as "sow", refers to any type of seed that is sown... notice the emphasis is placed on any type of seed, which applies to every area of life including both physical and spiritual... (and that which is just as important as the meaning itself) is the tense used in the Greek language

which means to continually and to habitually keep doing what you're doing over and over and over and over again... The reason most people walk away from the promises... is that they never really put it to test... they sowed once, waited, and nothing happened. So they threw up their arms and said, " It did not work"!... but those who keep on habitually sowing will reap and reap and reap!"

In other words, giving is not something we do, but rather is a lifestyle which expresses who we are in Christ. For example, I have personally lived this type of lifestyle of tithing and giving offerings for years, and can testify of the many times when we were supernaturally blessed as a result. The truth of the matter is, one cannot outgive God. He reciprocates what is given back to Him to those who have a humble and contrite heart. We need to understand that there is a set time for harvest for every type of seed we sow, and those who sow any type of seed properly will receive back a return of a 30, 60, or 100-fold increase over what they give. Hallelujah! God is good!

In previous chapters, we have considered the necessity of seeking God's presence daily, making it the most important appointment of the day. We know that He desires our company and fellowship, and He desires to speak with us. We need to understand that the words we speak are a type of seed, whether they are God's words or our own. Sitting and listening to Jesus was never intended to be the full extent of our relationship with Him. There is a lot more to Kingdom life than sitting still in a perpetual Kum Ba Yah state as we experience Holy Ghost goosebumps. He puts His seed in our heart for us to nurture and act upon!

Waiting on the Lord is the launching pad for action, not

the end in itself. His intent is to give His servants personal instruction, direction, and equipping which will germinate into the spread of the Kingdom of God on earth. Remember, our destiny has never been about being spectators sitting on bleachers waving pompoms and cheering, "Go Jesus go!" Mankind was placed in the Garden of Eden to dress it, which means to go to work with the seeds and tools God has given us. God's program is for us to actively hear what He says, lay it to heart, and then act in cultivating His garden.

THE COMMANDMENT TO GOD'S PRIESTS: RECEIVE THE SEED INTO YOUR HEART

> *And now, O ye priests, this commandment is for you. If ye will ... hear, and if ye will... lay it to heart,...to give glory to My name...*
>
> — MALACHI 2:1-2

Nowhere in the Bible are we told that we are to live a life of moderation in our relationship with Jesus. He is Lord, period! He is always looking for those who come to fellowship with Him who are saying, "Yes Lord, I will obey", even before He ever says anything to us. He is not our personal guru who gives us good vibes and optional self-help instructions to follow if we so desire. Whatever we hear Him speaking or see Him doing, that is what we are commanded to do. We must make a predetermined, sold-out decision in our heart to obey Him, regardless, as one who is on fire to serve Jesus Christ. Our lives are not our own!

In lieu of this, let's take a moment to consider the importance of Malachi 2 in waiting upon Him as our Lord. In this last book of the Old Testament, the Bible narrative continues concerning mankind's assignment of expanding the Kingdom of God on planet earth. From the influences of the fall of man in the Garden of Eden, mankind's assignment was rendered impossible to complete! However, God has never deviated from His original intent, which is that mankind is destined to be a race of His priests. We were created to live faithfully in His service in accomplishing this endeavor.

God's nation of priests was given the means to be successful through properly managing three types of seeds. However, mankind became helpless to execute this destiny until Jesus Christ cried out, " It is finished". He died on the cross and rose from the dead in 33 AD, which activated His ministry of reconciliation, a mission of reset which reestablished divine order as intended at creation. Mankind, through living in Christ, can now accomplish God's original intent of creation.

In Malachi 1:1-2, we see that the principles dealing with the relationship between God and man as based upon the Hebrew word BARAK are still valid. Nowhere in the Bible does this change. Indeed, this truth carries over to the life of the New Testament believers. Simply put, God expects us to listen with the intent to hear and to obey. When we are obedient, we will be blessed. When we are disobedient, we will suffer the consequences. What we sow, we reap.

In Malachi 2:2 the Hebrew word SHAMA is translated[3] as "hear" and means for someone to hear intelligently, and takes on the connotation of obedience in certain contexts. Also, it means to heed a request or a command. This should be our intent when we approach His throne as His servant.

Upon hearing God's word, we are told to "lay it to heart". The Hebrew word SUM is translated as "lay" and means that we are to receive His message into our heart. How do we do this? There are six different ways[4]:

- First, by hearing His voice and laying it to heart, we will come out of darkness into the Kingdom of light. We become citizens of His Kingdom! When we are born again, He makes all things new.
- The second meaning is to appoint people to their proper position of authority in life as overcomers. God gives His people crowns for the things of the world that they overcome.
- The third meaning is to establish a new relationship, as we are enabled to enter a covenant relationship with Christ.
- The fourth meaning is to assign something to someone, which is realized as God gives us work to do.
- The fifth meaning is to bring about a change in a person. We are transformed into a new creature as we repent from sin and turn to live for Him.
- The sixth meaning is to set aside something or someone for a special purpose. We experience this when we realize and are separated to our personal destiny.

What can I expect if I hear and lay it to heart? Malachi 2:4-9 tells us exactly what we should expect. God's life will begin to flow forth from us and will impact others! The law of truth, His words, will be spoken by our mouth, and we will no longer be comfortable speaking words like those spoken in the world.

We are empowered with wisdom and righteous judgment in the affairs of life. Our lives will be a living testimony of the goodness of God, and as a result, we will see people convicted of their sins and turn to God. People will be drawn to us for answers to the problems in our culture as they recognize that we have the goods as the messengers of God. All of this is done through the enabling power of Holy Spirit as we listen to what He says and live our lives accordingly in Christ. This is our destiny as a priest of God!

In Malachi 2:1, the priest of God is to "glorify His Name". The Hebrew word used for this phrase means to show[5] God the honor He deserves. Please consider that everything that the priest of God does is based upon His directions and provision, which in turn brings forth action. Our actions should stem from whatever His idea is, with His anointing and resources being provided to get it done. Therefore, God deserves all the glory every time.

SHAMAR: Application of Hearing and Laying to Heart

> *And the LORD God took the man, and put him into the garden of Eden to dress it and to keep it.*
>
> — Genesis 2:15

If you recall, God put our ancestors to work and He expects us to work as well. In Genesis 2:15, the Hebrew word SHAMAR is used[6] for the phrase, "keep it" which means to hedge about, to guard, to protect, or to attend to something. It also means to stay awake at night as a watchman. In the horticultural context of usage, this word means to use tools to break up the ground; to remove weeds, rocks, and debris; to add amendments and fertilizer to the soil; sow the seeds; water and maintain moisture in the ground; make sure the plot receives proper light from the sun; and give the appropriate amount of time required from germination to the harvest. From a military standpoint, this horticultural process is to be done while simultaneously being vigilant in protecting the harvest from predators and enemies.

Every Hebrew word indicates a mental picture of an action of some sort, which differs in this sense from most words in English. Inherent within the meaning of SHAMAR is the aspect of each of us taking personal responsibility for what we are supposed to do. The buck stops here! We are the one given charge to bring forth the harvest, in the right way, and in the right location as ordered by God. It must be guarded as well. We are required to wait, or watch, over every step of the cultivation process to nurture our garden, and to be a watchman to protect against enemies and danger.

Some additional aspects of our personal responsibility include understanding that there is a geographical dynamic defining the boundaries, location, and people group God assigns for our mission. On a personal level, we are to keep our word to our own hurt, to faithfully discharge the responsibilities of our office, and to keep our obligations. We are to keep our mouth by being prudent in the words we speak. Also, embedded in the meaning of SHAMAR, is that we are to follow the dictates of prudence, justice, kindness, and wisdom. As you can see, this is a very important word for believers to understand and apply. God did not make any benchwarmers! We have work we are responsible to do!

Let's take a moment and contrast the Biblical narrative of a nation of working priests of God, which we have been studying, with the teachings of many Western churches today. The author Kyle Idelman[7] had this to say,

"It may seem there are many followers of Jesus, but if they were honestly to define the relationship with Him I'm not sure it would be accurate to describe them as followers. It seems to me that there is a more suitable word to describe them,... as, " an enthusiastic admirer". I think Jesus has a lot of fans these days... who know nothing of sacrifice and pain. Many of our Churches today in America have gone from being sanctuaries to becoming stadiums. Every week all the fans come to the stadium where they cheer for Jesus but have no interest in truly following him... they want to be close enough to Jesus to get all the benefits, but not so close that it requires anything from them."

It is appropriate to restate, Yield To Yield is a book for those who are serious about having a vibrant, living relationship with Jesus. Each of us has the freedom of choice. You can be an admirer of Christ, or you can be a disciple of Christ. There is a price required of a disciple, which is to give up all aspects of our life and to become like our Lord. There is no place for compromise in this decision.

When a person hears God's word and lays it to heart, he becomes the SHAMAR of God. It is not by chance that the root of SHAMAR is SHAMA. One immediately recognizes from the definition of SHAMA (to hear properly), that listening carefully is inherent in the definition of the word SHAMAR. We must first become the field where God's word, or seed, is planted as we listen. When this seed germinates at salvation, it begins to grow as we water it with the Word and worship. If we continue to do the things necessary to grow spiritually, we will become increasingly like Him and will produce the fruit of the Kingdom.

In other words, we become the SHAMAR of God before we can increase the Kingdom in the world. SHAMAR is both a state of being and an active process. That is, the person's heart acts as a field, His word is a living seed, and a harvest of the Kingdom is brought forth in our lives. At that point, the Kingdom will flow forth from the heart to influence others. Everything starts with the internal work of Holy Spirt, and the overflow impacts our lives as well as those in our sphere of influence.

After we receive the seed of His word in our heart and are born again, we are to cultivate and water our hearts with worship, Bible study, fellowship with believers at Church and other places, and separation from the lifestyle of sin. Over the process of time, we will begin to reap the fruit of the Kingdom in our life. Only then will we be enabled to take the Kingdom to sow into our families, the Church, and ultimately to the people and systems of the world.

The Laws Governing Sowing and Reaping

> *And God said, Let the earth bring forth grass, the herb yielding seed,* and *the fruit tree yielding fruit after his kind, whose seed is in itself, upon the earth: and it was so.*
>
> — Genesis 1:11-12

On the third day of creation, God defined and established the law which applies to all aspects of seed management and harvest. This law governs the management and the behavior of all types of seeds. God said, let the earth bring forth seed that would bear after its kind. This deals with the nature and potential that is in every type of seed. In this context, this means that as the seed germinates and becomes a plant, it will always be just like the plant that produced the fruit that the seed came from. Like produces like, and therefore there is a continuance of this same type of plant into the future. This is foundational to our understanding of the other aspects governing the cultivation of seeds as presented in the Bible. Keeping this in mind, let's consider other aspects of this law.

1. The Law of Sowing and Reaping Rules Every Type of Seed

There are different seeds for all the different plant groups on planet earth, but there are also seeds of the body, or procreation; the seed of increase, or the work of production of our hands; and the seed of rule, which deals with what we worship as evidenced by the words which come out of our heart. The same Law applies to natural seed management as well as the supernatural seeds which are directly related to the life of man. Therefore, God's people must understand how to bear the proper fruit, after its kind, in the words we speak, in how we raise our children, and in how we steward over what we produce from managing the land.

2. This Law is Applied as a Process Involving Both Time and Diligence

In Ecclesiastes 11:6, we learn that there is a process involving time and diligence in the management of seeds. If we do not work, we will not eat. This is especially true as we arrive at the time of the harvest. There is work required to plant seeds and to cultivate them until they are ready to bear fruit. However, as mentioned in Job 39:12, there is a set time for the harvest. I personally understand the hard work of the harvest required from years of having my own garden. The harvest always requires more work than any other stage of the growing season.

3. Some Seed is Bread and Some Seed is for us to Replant

In Second Corinthians 9:8-10, we learn that God gives us seed to sow in order to produce bread and more seed. God gives us our bread for us to eat and to meet our needs. It is our portion! God wants to bless us and provide for us. But also, there is a portion of the seed that is to be set aside to be sown again which we are not to eat. We must be very careful not to eat our seed. Keep in mind that our bread is to meet our current needs, while our seed is to be used to meet our future needs.

4. God Reserves a Portion of a Harvest For Himself

In Joshua 6:17, we observe an example of the truth that part of every harvest belongs to God, and is to be set aside for Him alone. In this case God claimed the tenth part of the cities in the promised land as sacrifice to Him. That which is to be set apart for Him, is not our portion to eat as our bread, but it is a part we sacrifice as we thank Him for blessing us. The Hebrew word for this is CHERUM which means[8] the accursed thing. It is a devoted thing to God marked for destruction. Personal sacrifice is required in the management of the three seeds in the following ways:

- We are to give tithes and offerings, instead of selfishly spending everything that we make, plus creating debt, from our seed of increase;
- We are to maintain chaste behavior reserving sexual intimacy exclusively for the marriage covenant, instead of engaging multiple sexual partners, in managing the seed of the body;
- We are to consistently speak words of faith and life, and not of doubt or unbelief, in managing the seed of rule.

5. The Death of a Seed Brings New Life

As a part of our sacrifice to the Lord we must learn to die to our own agendas, feelings, and emotions. This means that we have to become a giver and not a taker, and we are to sacrifice our resources, talents, and time as He leads. We are to continually speak about the testimony of Jesus Christ in our lives. Whenever a seed is planted, the death of the seed occurs, which brings forth new life as it germinates.

6. People Plant Seeds in Everything That They Do

Finally, mankind plants either good seed or bad seed in every endeavor he undertakes. In I Peter 1:23, there are seeds that are corruptible which are of darkness and death which are based upon the Adamic nature. On the other hand, there are the incorruptible seeds that are the Word of God which live and abide forever. Whether we realize it or not, a person will reap from whatever type of seed that he or she has sown.

The Law which governs sowing and reaping has been revealed to us by God for our benefit and prosperity. If we ignore this law, it may be at our own peril. This is a matter of life and death, and the choice is up to us.

New Testament Aspects of Seed Management

By this point you probably realize that it is the author's opinion that no one accomplishes his Kingdom destiny because of a charming personality, talents, or good looks. Anyone building life on this foundation may experience temporary results, but nothing of lasting value will ever remain. This is true as well of those who are living a life of quiet desperation, hanging onto the hope that one day their ship will come into the harbor. The Kingdom of God does not increase as a matter of random chance. On the contrary, destiny is achieved by those who hear, lay it to heart, and then do it! This is the script! This starts with the smallest seed of His word in your heart which germinates and begins to change you into an overcoming man or woman of God.

Jesus Taught Us How the Kingdom is to Grow

> *"I speak to you timeless truth. The Son is not able to do anything from Himself or through My own initiative. I only do the works that I see the Father doing, for the Son does the same works as His Father."*

— JOHN 5:19

Let's look further at Jesus' teaching on the subject of sowing and reaping in respect to the growth potential of the seeds of the Kingdom.

> *Jesus also told them this parable: "God's kingdom realm is like someone spreading seed on the ground. The farmer goes to bed and gets up, day after day, and the seed sprouts and grows tall, though he knows not how. All by itself it sprouts, and the soil produces a crop; first the green stem, then the head on the stalk, and then the fully developed grain in the head. Then, when the grain is ripe, he immediately puts the sickle to the grain, because harvest time has come."*
>
> — MARK 4:26-29

In this scripture Jesus was making it plain that when one spreads seeds onto the ground, it is always done in faith that there will be a harvest. Most farmers have no real understanding of what germination or growth really are, but they know it requires a process that takes hard work, time, and patience. Our role in managing Kingdom seed is to sow it into good ground and apply faith that the harvest will come. We need to understand that God is responsible to bring the increase, not us. This is the nature and order of the Kingdom of God.

> *Then Jesus taught them another parable: "Heaven's kingdom realm can be compared to the tiny mustard seed that a man takes and plants in his field. Although the smallest of all the seeds, it eventually grows into the greatest of garden plants, becoming a tree for birds to come and build their nests in its branches."*
>
> — MATTHEW 13:31-32

The type of mustard seed plant described in this verse[9] is an indigenous species of the Middle East area. This scripture presents the pervasive nature of how the Kingdom of God grows. The seed of this plant is very small, but when planted, properly cultivated, and nurtured, it flourishes to grow to a large size and produces much fruit. For our purposes, this exemplifies the continuous ongoing faith we are to apply when planting and managing the three seeds of the Kingdom. Never despise small beginnings. The management of spiritual seeds is reflected in the management of physical seeds. In both cases, the fruit we produce will be food for the nations.

> *Then he taught them another parable: "Heaven's kingdom realm can be compared to yeast that a woman takes and blends into three measures of flour and then waits until all the dough rises."*
>
> — MATTHEW 13:33

This scripture also illuminates the growth potential and the nature of the Kingdom of God. Again, we are not to despise small beginnings. Most of the time, the seeds we plant will generally be very small, but over time their impact will increase in size and in scope. Remember, mankind's original assignment was to take a very small area called the Garden of Eden, or paradise, and to increase it to cover the entire world. This is the growth potential of the seeds of the Kingdom.

SUMMATION

Mankind was established for the purpose of carrying God's image and likeness to earth. We were created to be a nation of priests. Each of us is a vessel He desires to carry the seeds of the Kingdom of God in expanding the Garden of Eden, or paradise, into spiritually desolate and dark places.

So far in our study, we have determined the daily necessity of approaching God as we bow to our Lord and Master. This is embodied in the meaning of the Hebrew word BARAK. As we bow at the throne, God gives us instructions and equips us to effectively manage three types of seeds. This management is designed to be done through a process, as defined by the Hebrew word SHAMAR. Directly related to this is the Law of Sowing and Reaping, which affects all aspects of seed management and must be carefully adhered to.

MEMORY SCRIPTURE

2 Corinthians 9:6-7 But this I say, He which soweth sparingly shall reap also sparingly; and he which soweth bountifully shall reap also bountifully. Every man according as he purposeth in his heart, so let him give; not grudgingly, or of necessity: for God loveth a cheerful giver.

QUESTIONS TO PONDER

1. Biblically, how does your heart compare to a garden?
2. How does the Hebrew word SHAMAR relate to fulfilling the purpose of your life?
3. How do you sow and reap from everything you do?

WHAT GOD SAYS ABOUT YOU

Write your answers in a notebook.

1. Read Matthew 13:1-43- Write down everything you learn about cultivation of seed in your heart.
2. Reread the section in this chapter on the usage of the Hebrew words SHAMAR and SHAMA- write how they apply to your life.
3. Reread the section in this scripture on the Law of Sowing and Reaping- write down the six main points and the actions that you should take as a result.

BECOMING WHO GOD CREATED YOU TO BE

1. Read Genesis 1:28; Mathew 28:19-20; Mark 16:15-20- Confess daily that your mission today is to plant good seed.
2. Add to your daily discipline- To determine to be

constantly aware of opportunities to sow good seed into people.
3. Meditate upon the fact that the more time that you spend with the Lord, the more seed and overflow of the anointing you will have to sow into the lives of others.

Chapter Seven
Shamar: Law of Unity

"The Church is everywhere represented as one. It is one body, one family, one-fold, one kingdom. It is one because it is pervaded by one Spirit. We are all baptized into one Spirit to become, says the apostle, one body."

— Charles Hodge

"Till we all come in the unity of the faith, and of the knowledge of the Son of God, unto a perfect man, unto the measure of the stature of the fulness of Christ..."

— Ephesians 4:13

As I sat on the bench while coaching our boys' basketball team, I looked at the scoreboard and realized we were behind by 60 points. And, we still had a quarter to play! The other team was well on their way to defending their 2nd state championship in as many years. Meanwhile, it was our first season fielding a varsity basketball team for our school. We were way overmatched as we fielded a very young team made up of junior high kids and one tenth grader, but we had some athletic ability on the team. I recognized that we had the problem of being inexperienced.

As a result, we would have some hard knocks along the way. But this would be overcome as we played more games. But more importantly, we were playing as individuals instead of playing as a team. As one would expect, we had not won a game nor were we very competitive. I vividly remember that moment as I looked at the floor of the basketball court asking God, "Are we ever going to win a game?"

After the basketball game against the state champs, God began to speak to me about our team strengths and what to do. Let me mention this right here, that God does not care which team wins a ball game, and that I have never prayed for the team to win. However, God is absolutely interested in every player that is on every team. So yes, God does care about a sports team or event from that perspective.

For the purpose of this book, it is important for you to take note of the following sequence of events. In 1986, God had given me the assignment of starting a Christian school, which included the development of our athletic program. I obeyed. I was exactly where God had assigned me to be, ministering to the kids that He had brought into my sphere of influence.

He had told me that my purpose was to raise up a generation to serve Jesus, which is still my destiny today. So, for me to begin to receive revelation for something as seemingly insignificant as coaching a boys basketball team was totally what I expected.

God began to speak to me about what to do with the basketball team. We had a team strength of quickness, and our guards were good athletes even though they were young. Our boys were not afraid to work hard. In addition, God showed me some things we could do to get our boys to play together as a team. As a result of His revelation, our practices became focused on installing a half court zone press, which at the time was not used by many teams. We practiced it until they were dreaming about it at night. Everyone knew their role and how to run it, and it turned our group of individuals into a team as we began to play together in unity.

During that time, I arranged a team trip to go watch a live SEC basketball game at Auburn University. In that game, Auburn ran a half court zone press with great success. This was a God thing! Honestly, when I made the arrangements, I did not know what defensive scheme Auburn ran. For such a time as this! The kids immediately recognized what Auburn was running and realized that maybe Coach knew what he was talking about after all.

At that moment, the kids fully bought into the team concept. They entered into unity as a team! What had been a difficult non-competitive season turned around immediately. Most teams had never seen the defense we ran, and it resulted in a lot of turnovers with a lot of easy layups. The team won the last 4 games of the season against teams that had beaten us badly earlier in the year. It was all God!

The Priest of God and the Law of Unity

> *Behold, how good and how pleasant* it is *for brethren to dwell together in unity!* It is *like the precious ointment upon the head, that ran down upon the beard,* even *Aaron's beard: that went down to the skirts of his garments; As the dew of Hermon,* and as the dew *that descended upon the mountains of Zion: for there the LORD commanded the blessing,* even *life for evermore.*

— Psalm 133:1-3

Psalm 133 is a very short chapter in the Bible, but one that contains great revelation for the enquiring student of the Word. That is, without His anointed direction and blessings in our life, we cannot accomplish His will. Therefore, it is important for us to understand and to walk in the revelation in Psalm 133, which the author calls the Law of Unity.

"May I have your attention please!" This is essentially how Psalm 133 begins with the exhortation to, "Behold...". The Hebrew word[1] this is translated from means, for us to fix our eyes upon a revealed truth, be sure to focus with all our attention, and/or to take care and observe what is about to be revealed. Obviously, there must be something of great importance if Holy Spirit has so moved the psalmist to begin the scripture in this way. In other words, there are truths in this scripture that will shock you. So pay attention and don't miss it!

The Hebrew word translated "good" and as "precious" in

verses 1-2, means that something is functionally good, and refers to the pristine condition of creation in Genesis 1. This is the goodness that only flows from God's divine nature and character, and implies that this goodness is still available to us after creation. His goodness takes many forms and can be tangible or intangible. Often His people receive His goodness in practical, economic, or material ways, and there is always a beneficial element which is made available to His people. God's heart is to bless each of us, and we are told that all His thoughts are for our good and for our prosperity.

God loves us! This is His default setting, not the anger or wrath that are unleashed upon the disobedient as mentioned in the Bible. As a result of His lovingkindness, He wants to give each of us that which is beautiful, best, precious, and bountiful. However, He is a God of wrath and judgement to those who continue to walk in iniquity and in wickedness. Even in God's dealings with the wicked, He gives plenty of time and opportunity for them to turn and to repent of their wicked ways before He visits them in their sin.

On the other hand, He is well pleased with those who are diligent seekers of His presence and who desire to be His faithful and obedient servants. This has nothing to do with whether we are deserving or worthy to receive such, because we never will be. God loves us! And the result will be that the nations will take note of how He blesses us and will come seeking us to receive such blessings for themselves.

Please take note that the blessings of God are not a matter of pure happenstance. We may all experience the benefits of His promises which flow forth from God when certain conditions are met. In this scripture, we are to, "dwell together in unity with our brethren". The Hebrew word translated[2] "brethren" refers to someone who is a blood relative or is related to us spiritually. Of course, there is power in the blood! Believers have a common bloodline through our Lord Jesus Christ our elder brother in the family of God. Understanding our relationship with Jesus is critical to having a relationship with Father God. Directly related to this concept is the use of the Hebrew word translated[3] as, "dwell together", which means to be married for life, or to be in covenant relationship with them.

Call to Come into Unity

Revelation of how God's people may gain access to His blessings are given in Psalm 133. This begins in verse one with the Hebrew word translated[4] as "unity", which means to be as one, or to unite together. In the Ancient Hebrew Lexicon of the Bible, the mental picture given by the Hebrew word is of a door that is in a wall. A wall separates whatever is on the inside from whatever is outside. Only through the door can one enter or exit to access and unite the inside with the outside.

Apparently, if God's people are in unity with Him, and with themselves, there is a door made which provides access to the blessings of the Lord. In summarizing verse one in today's English,

"Take a close look because you will be surprised to learn that God's intent is to give you every good thing you need in life to fulfill your purpose if you understand and obey His Law of Unity. As a part of this, a door of access to the blessings will be made to those in unity."

It is the author's opinion, as based upon experience, that there is a Law of Unity which exists. When adhered to, it will bring forth the manifestation of, "on earth as it is in heaven". We already know that the New Testament believer is to be "in (unity with) Christ", which is the initial condition required for this law to operate. There are principles associated with this law that are essential for us to follow. This has nothing to do with our personal salvation, but it has everything to do with being successful in our assignment on earth. These principles are uncovered as mysteries of God's Kingdom in the other verses of Psalm 133.

On a practical level, the Law of Unity is to be applied in the management of the three types of seeds God gives us to expand the Kingdom of God. In addition, we will learn that this Law impacts five different types of relationships in our lives.

We are given the task of being in unity in every area of our life. This starts within us as we bring our body, soul, and spirit into proper order. Then, it expands to include our eternal covenant with God. After this, we establish our progeny for the continuance and future growth of the Kingdom of God. After we are faithful in the first three areas, we increase our sphere of influence in being an active and productive member in the local church God places us in. Finally, we bring the individuals we know who are not saved into unity with us through the foolishness of preaching. Also, we influence all the systems of the culture in education, business, religion, government, etc., in bringing them into unity with the principles of the Kingdom of God. If we do this, we will turn the world upside down even as the first century Apostles did.

We will further define these five fields in our life in greater detail in the next chapter.

Source of the Anointing

In Psalm 133:2 *It is* like the precious ointment upon the head, that ran down upon the beard, *even* Aaron's beard: that went down to the skirts of his garments...

The word translated[5] as "ointment" is a very significant word for believers. This word is used in the sense of being rich or fat. The scripture draws a parallel between the blessings we experience from being in proper unity in all areas of life, to the anointing oil which was poured upon the high priest at his ordination ceremony. Aaron was the high priest of God, the head of the Church, or the leading spiritual authority. The High Priest represents God-ordained authority.

Identify God-Ordained Authority

The first practical application[6] of the Law of Unity is that we are to walk circumspectly in every situation of life. In the process, we are to properly identify the God-ordained, God-blessed, and God anointed authority that is present. There are times when there is no God-ordained authority present. In such times we must be led by Holy Spirit. He may require us to pray silently or out loud, in the spirit or with understanding. He may lead us to speak to someone of the Gospel of the Kingdom, of words of life and of encouragement, or of blessings. Holy Spirit may lead us to take a stand in offering physical protection to the weak or the helpless. Whatever the Lord requires of us will influence the situation with the Kingdom of God. We become His authority in that situation.

God will never break our will but calls us to voluntarily submit to His authority. Our submission to someone should not be based on personality, good looks, or talents, but must be directly related to the call and anointing of God on the person's life. We are not to judge by the standards of the world, but rather by the leading of Holy Spirit. This is not that difficult to do once we realize that as we submit to and serve authority, God's blessings will be released in our life.

THE SEED OF THE KINGDOM

In Psalm 133:2 we have already discussed some of the aspects of, ..."the precious ointment". Let's examine the Hebrew word SHEMEN which is translated[7] as "ointment", and means to shine, to glory, or to be oily. This Hebrew word is where we get our English word semen, which is a type of seed. A mental picture is given of the flow of anointing oil dripping down unto the garments of the high priest. The word translated as "head" means the chief or leader of a person, place, or time, and refers to any type of authority which is present at any given time. The mental picture presented is of the seed of God, which is the source of all life, being poured out upon the head of authority. in every situation and in every circumstance.

UNITY PRINCIPLES TO FOLLOW: PRACTICAL APPLICATION

Let's consider the practical application of what has been revealed so far in Psalm 133. We will use the Law of Unity to our benefit as we apply the following principles in submitting to authority. This is a lifestyle issue! Please keep in mind that these principles should habitually be applied as a matter of our daily self-discipline.

We have already considered the first two principles:

1. <u>Look for God's authority</u>: In every situation and every area of life, we need to identify the authority that is present. We need to be aware that some have usurped authority for evil or selfish purposes. In such cases, they have disqualified themselves.
2. <u>Sometimes God may appoint you as His authority</u>: There is authority present in every situation. Sometimes I will be the set man. However, most of the time it will be someone else. I must learn to submit myself to authority, in order to be an authority. Whatever I sow, I will reap.

Let's continue in our consideration of additional principles. Psalm 133:2 includes the phrase, "...ran down the beard, even Aaron's beard..."

During the ordination ceremony of the High Priest, the oil of anointing was poured upon the head and allowed to run freely across his face to eventually drip from his beard. The beard represents the moving of the chin as a person speaks, which symbolizes God's anointing being on the words which are spoken by His authority. The seed of rule, which is a matter of the heart, is revealed through the words which are spoken. God's anointing drips freely upon the words spoken by His anointed man.

It is important to determine to listen intently when an authority speaks. For example, I worked as an associate chaplain at a local hospital for 20 years. We had several different people who served as the head chaplain over the course of those years. All the chaplain staff were in full-time ministry, and each one was more gifted or dynamic in at least one area than everyone else. Any of us could have done a great job. During our staff meetings, there was never a shortage of opinions or suggestions of how to do something. But only one person could lead. Whatever the head chaplain decided, that was what we did, and we strove to do it with excellence even though we may not have agreed with the decision.

We must have childlike faith that the set man has spent time with God and has been given divine guidance. We are all capable of hearing God.

However, we must be very careful who we listen to. The Bible teaches that there are many voices in the world and we will have to deal with false teachers and prophets in the Church, as well as those who serve darkness in secular institutions. I have found that in situations where I am unfamiliar with the authority, that Holy Spirit will reveal whether they serve God or not if I pray and ask. Also, Holy Spirit gives me an "impression of uneasiness" when I am around someone who is a counterfeit or has major spiritual problems.

> 3. Listen to what the authority says: I must actively seek to hear the directions given by an authority in order to line up with the Law of Unity and to accomplish God's purpose. There are many voices in the world, but we are to hear and to recognize only the voice of Kingdom authority.

As we continue to study[8] Psalm 133:2, the phrase " went down to the skirts of his garments" is used. The skirts referred to the linen robes worn by the priest. The Hebrew word for "skirts", is PAAH. In addition, the word "garments" refers[9] to that which covers. The root word of this means to blow away, or to puff. The Bible teaches that Holy Spirit is the RUACH, or breath/wind of God. This Hebrew word brings forth a mental picture of the breath of God coming under the robe, filling it with air, and puffing it out.

God is a God of order and of government. The linen robe which covered the body of the High Priest is a reflection of how God-ordained government acts as a covering to protect the people. As a result, the people are empowered to act in unity as one Body accomplishing the work of the Kingdom. Meanwhile, God's anointing manifests as it drips from the chin, the words spoken, and lands on the garment which is the governmental protection for the people. At that point, the Holy Spirit wind blows upon the government and the people under its covering. This wind is the manifest presence of God which ministers with, and through, His people in meeting the needs of the nations.

The Law of Unity is triggered when God's people enter and remain in proper relationship to His authority. This Law operates from the most elementary level to the most impersonal and universal levels. In other words, all areas of our lives are directly impacted by our faithfulness in obeying the Law of Unity.

> 4. <u>God anoints His authority with His vision, and He raises up others to help him accomplish it:</u> There is only one right way where things will work properly for a given situation. This is based on the God-given vision of His government in the form of an authority's vision. We are to carefully listen to to the vision. Follow those directions carefully. Often there are several ways to accomplish something, but only one way will work best.
> 5. <u>The Law of Unity operates from the most personal</u>

level (body, soul, and spirit) to the most impersonal levels in life (government and culture).
6. The Law of Unity is activated by God's people remaining in proper relationship with Him and in proper relationship with the person He sets in authority.

In the last verse in Psalm 133:3, the phrase "as the dew of Hermon" is used. This refers to an unusual mist that often rises from the Mediterranean Sea and settles onto Mount Hermon during the dry season. This mist gives moisture to the snowcap, replenishes the springs, and waters all the mountain plants. This mist covers the mountainside with moisture which eventually flows down the slopes to the plains below to water the crops, the lilies of the fields, and the grass for flocks to graze on. This natural phenomenon blesses the people.[10]

Psalm 133:3, gives us the perfect mental picture of the nature of the blessings that unity brings forth. These blessings are always more than enough for what we need. The scripture ends with the phrase, "for there the Lord commands the blessings". Please note that the blessings are conditional! The blessings of God come upon those who enter and remain in a state of unity. Whenever the proper conditions of unity are met, God proclaims the blessings to be loosed into that situation.

Psalm 133 concludes with, "...there is where the Lord commands the blessing...". The root of the Hebrew word used for "blessing" is BARAK, and in this case refers to a man that is blessed and happy.

7. The blessings of God come on those who identify and voluntarily submit themselves to authority: The blessings are a consequence of our submission in

helping accomplish the vision of the set man. We do not have to strive for them.

8. <u>The blessings of God are conditional</u>: We are required to meet the proper criteria in dealing with the God-ordained authority in our lives as a part of properly seeing and hearing what He is telling His servants to do. Often our authority will confirm what the Lord is already showing us.

In summarizing the principles related to the Law of Unity, please be aware that this law is predicated upon each of us, including those in authority, to spend time daily in waiting upon the Lord. This is foundational and is a matter of habit and of self-discipline. Please be mindful that the Biblical definition of success is obedience. To not hear what He has to say and to not obey His vision will lead to defeat in our lives, whether we are born again or not. If we listen and obey, God will tell us where to go, who to serve, and what to do.

The Law of Unity is not the total answer of how one is to be a priest king of God. It is one of the key components. However, I believe that as you combine the other elements presented in this book with the Law of Unity, you will be well on your way down the right path to fulfilling your destiny.

MEMORY SCRIPTURE

Romans 13:1-4 Let every soul be subject unto the higher powers. For there is no power but of God: the powers that be are ordained of God. Whosoever resists the power, resists the ordinance of God: and they that resist shall receive to themselves damnation. For rulers are not a terror to good works, but to the evil. Will you then not be afraid of the power? Do that which is good, and you will have praise of the same: For he is the minister of God to your for good. But if you do that which is evil, be afraid; for he bears not the sword in vain: for he is the minister of God, a revenger to execute wrath upon him that does evil.

QUESTIONS TO PONDER

1. Have you accepted the fact that Jesus expects you to be His disciple, which requires you to make time to spend with Him daily?
2. Do you have a five-fold minister who is teaching you how to be in unity with the church?
3. Do you consistently submit to authority in every situation?

WHAT GOD SAYS ABOUT YOU

Write your answers in a notebook.

1. Reread the section in this chapter on the practical application of the Law of Unity- write down the eight ways to apply unity to every area of life.
2. Read Ephesians 4- write down the biblical role of the five-fold ministry in your life. Include how they impact sin that is in the heart of believers.
3. Read Romans 13- write down the aspects of God-ordained government and how they are to handle darkness, wickedness, and evil in men.

BECOMING WHO GOD CREATED YOU TO BE

1. Add to your daily discipline- humble yourself and determine to never take anyone else's glory as your own.
2. Discuss with your pastor or mentor the aspects of God-given authority and how it applies in all fields of relationship.
3. Determine daily to submit properly to authorities, and to lead biblically as you are called upon by men or by Holy Spirit.

Chapter Eight
Introduction to the Five Fields and The Field of Relationship of Our Body, Soul, and Spirit

I have seen many men work without praying, though I have never seen any good come out of it; but I have never seen a man pray without working.[1]

— Hudson Taylor

> *Not everyone that says unto me, Lord, Lord, shall enter into the kingdom of heaven; but he that does the will of my Father which is in heaven. Many will say to me in that day, Lord, Lord, have we not prophesied in your name... in your name have cast out devils... done many wonderful works? And then will I profess unto them, I never knew you: depart from me, you that work iniquity.*
>
> — Matthew 7:21-23

In the book of Matthew, Jesus made a rather disturbing statement as He issued a personal challenge to everyone who calls themselves a disciple of Christ. Stop and think about this! There are many paths you can take in life; therefore, you must be sure that you are on the right path to the Kingdom of God. Jesus says that many will be on the wrong path, even though they think the path they have chosen will lead to heaven.

What path are you on? Are you on the path that focuses on Jesus being only your Savior? Or, are you on a path where Jesus is Savior and Lord? Are you on a path of waiting for Him to bail you out of your troubles? Or, are you on a path to becoming the overcomer of your troubles?

Walk the Walk and Talk the Talk

Let's consider for a moment what the author Kyle Idleman wrote about this issue,

"...in verse 21 Jesus makes a distinction... we live in a time when we have become increasingly comfortable in separating what we say we believe with how we live. We have convinced ourselves that our beliefs are sincere even though they have no impact on how we live... biblical belief is more than something we confess with our mouth; it is something we confess with our lives."[2]

It is time for us to be real with God, to totally sell out our life to serve Him. I am not calling us into five-fold ministry, but I am recognizing His call to each of us to surrender totally to Him with our words as well as all the actions we take. Our destiny is to be a vessel of light standing in opposition to darkness. However, this will require us to change. The problem is that no one likes change!

The Altar Before the Throne

> *"...I saw also the Lord sitting upon a throne, high and lifted up, and his train filled the temple. Above it stood the seraphim... Then flew one of the seraphim unto me, having a live coal in his hand, which he had taken with the tongs from off the altar...*
>
> — Isaiah 6:1-2, 6

In Isaiah 6, the prophet Isaiah was given a vision of the throne of God in heaven. The throne of God was not the only thing he was shown. There were heavenly creatures called Seraphim who were stationed around the throne. Also, there was an altar before the throne. Wherever the throne of God is, there is an altar in proximity. Why an altar at the throne? God expects those who approach His throne to worship and sacrifice to Him. What does He want us to sacrifice? Everything in our lives!

> *I beseech you therefore, brethren, by the mercies of God, that ye present your bodies a living sacrifice, holy, acceptable unto God, which is your reasonable service. And be not conformed to this world: but be ye transformed by the renewing of your mind, that*

> *ye may prove what is that good, and acceptable, and perfect, will of God.*
>
> — Romans 12:1-2

As we approach the throne of God after we are born again, we come into the presence of absolute holiness and righteousness. All flesh trembles before His presence, and no sin can abide there. What this means to us in practical terms is that God immediately begins the process of cleaning up our lives. His intent is to change us from our old way of living into a new creature made in His image. We literally become like Christ!

Therefore, we should expect that as we wait upon the Lord, He will "get into our stuff". God takes each of us where we are, just as we are, and then begins to clean us up from the darkness we have lived in. For example, God deals with the issue of sin in our lives, as well as how we have been wronged (Hebrews 10:2). He commands us to renew our minds by reading the Bible. As we memorize, personalize and begin to live according to His Word, He transforms us into His image (2 Corinthians 10:2). Also, He deals with the lack of love in our hearts as He enables us to forgive past hurts and offenses. It is impossible for us to love others without first being able to love ourselves. This is by no means a complete list of how He changes us at His altar. However, the end result is that we are changed into a new creature.

Remember that Christianity has never been about deciding to ask Jesus into our heart. If this was merely about making a decision, we would be called "decision makers". Instead we are called Christians. This has always been about making disciples who are followers of Christ. There is a big difference between being a decision maker, and someone who is actively changing and becoming like Christ. As we become more and more like Him, we become more enabled to resist darkness.

> *When the enemy comes in like a flood, the Spirit of the Lord shall lift up a standard against him.*
>
> — Isaiah 59:19

The Hebrew word NUS is translated[3] as "standard", and gives us a mental picture of a seed, which represents the continuance of life. A second mental picture is of a thorn, which represents the idea of grabbing ahold of something. Combined these words mean, "continue to grab hold". Historically, the Church has been God's standard which is raised up to stand against the flood of wickedness in the world. For example, five centuries ago, He raised up the remnant Church to stand against the abuses of a false religious system. This resulted in the birth of the Reformation.

But how is God raising up this type of standard, which is the Church, and how is it supposed to work in today's world? The answer is in the practical usages and literal meaning of the Hebrew word NUS:

- We are being called to action.
- We are to be like a flag lifted high to be seen from a distance.
- We are to grab hold of our destiny and perform it as we take the seeds of the Kingdom into desolation.
- We are to lift up the load, or burden, of the Lord's calling on our lives and be faithful.[4]

- We are to be the vessels of light to those who dwell in darkness.

There is nothing passive about the definition[5] of the word "standard". In fact, it is the author's opinion that the remnant Church is being stirred today by Holy Spirit into action. This is a KAIROS moment! The Greek word KAIROS refers to a very specific point in time, which is a pivotal God-ordained point in history. God is calling us to arise and to act in opposition to darkness and evil in the world systems around us. God is equipping and enabling an army to wage war in His strength and power. As a result, the Church is destined to be more powerful than the storm of wickedness in this generation. The power of God is much greater than the power of hell. It is not even close! It is time for the Church to make a stand!

The balance of this book is dedicated to the fundamental discipline and habits necessary to becoming prepared and transformed into His remnant army. It is time for action! We have already focused on the foundational aspects of yielding ourselves to Him in previous chapters. We will now focus upon the practical daily application which directly results in yielding the fruit and harvest of the Kingdom. In this process, it is critical that we not lose sight of the foundation laid in earlier chapters.

Christianity is a life that is lived by those who exercise personal discipline. Disciples practice discipline. The two cannot be separated. I have observed that successful people tend to maintain habits, or self-discipline, which promotes their success. This is true regardless of your field of employment. Many people are seldom successful because they do not maintain the proper discipline. The revivalist T.L.Osborne once said, "You can take and place me anywhere in the world and I will still produce the fruit of the Kingdom of God." He was a man of great discipline who put his hands to work wherever he was. His faithfulness resulted in entire nations being turned upside down by the work of one man of God. Work is required! No discipline or habits will lead to success unless you work at it!

Reference for Understanding The Three Seeds and The Five Fields

The three seeds you manage represent aspects of your character and nature, as well as strongholds of thought. Once you are born again, you should change over time as you are transformed into a son of God.

1. The Seed of Rule (deals with the spirit of man)- is directly related to who you recognize, and submit to, as authority. This also includes how you show honor. This is reflected by the words you speak. When you serve God as your Master, you will consistently speak words of faith and life, and not of doubt or unbelief.
2. The Seed of the Body (deals with disciplining the flesh)- is directly related to how you manage procreation, to your perspective concerning the continuance of the human race, and to the value you place on life. You are to maintain chaste behavior by reserving sexual intimacy exclusively for marriage. This includes developing an eternal perspective to life, instead of living daily to satisfy your lusts. You are responsible to train your future generations to serve Jesus.

3. The Seed of Increase/Production (deals with the soul of man)- is directly related to how you create wealth and manage resources to meet your needs and the needs of others. This includes financing the growth of the Kingdom of God. You are to produce more than enough to meet your needs plus give tithes and offerings as a type of worship. This contrasts with the pattern of spending every dime you make, plus going into debt, to selfishly fulfill your lusts and temptations. Also, this includes worshiping and praising God in song and musical instruments accompanied by clapping, shouting, dance, etc., in your personal devotional time as well as in church services.

The five fields are symbols of the different types of relationships you have in your life. The three seeds are to be properly sown into each of these relationships. The Fields of Relationship are:

- Field #1- The relationship of your body, soul, and spirit within yourself: This field deals with the government of our soul, or how we are to think. We sow good or bad seed to this field by what we see with our eyes.
- Field #2- The relationship you have with God: This field deals with the government of your spirit, or of how you live. Worship and praise are important, and we are transformed into a giver.
- Field #3- The relationship you have with family: This field deals with the government of the body, and how we are to relate to other people.

- Field #4- The relationship you have with the Church: This field deals with the government of belonging, or how I am to serve in the Church.
- Field #5- The relationship with the World: This field deals with the government of your individual purpose, and of spreading the Gospel of the Kingdom of God. The proper government in this field determines how you deal with relationships in the marketplace and influence business, education, etc., with the Kingdom of God.

How these Fields relate to each other:

- We experience personal growth incrementally, starting with first field of personal relationship and progressing to the largest in Field #5.
- As we experience growth in each field, we are enabled to grow in the subsequent fields.
- There are no shortcuts. For example, we must first grow in the field within ourselves by being born again. Then we are enabled to grow in the field of our relationship with God.
- Each successive field represents an increasing sphere of influence.
- We must learn how to serve God and others.

The Five Fields

Field #1- The Relationship of Our Body, Soul and Spirit Within Ourself: This field deals with the government of our soul, or how we are to think. We sow good or bad seed to this field by what we see with our eyes.

There are four major aspects of how we cultivate the relationship of our body, soul, and spirit, within ourselves. First, we must be born again and need to be baptized in Holy Spirit. Second, we learn how to wait upon the Lord. Third, we learn the discipline of renewing our minds. And finally, we learn how to speak properly. But before we discuss these four main aspects, let's consider this field from the standpoint of God's original intent at creation.

Original Intent:

> *And the LORD God formed man of the dust of the ground, and breathed into his nostrils the breath of life; and man became a living soul.*
>
> — Genesis 2:7

When God created man He formed him from the dust. The Hebrew word translated[6] as "dust" gives us a mental picture of the fine shavings of flammable wood or kindling that one users to start a fire. God made man of the earth and gave him dominion over the earth. But He also made man to be ignited by the consuming fire of His presence. Mankind is the chosen vessel to carry the fire of God.

God also made mankind a living soul. Adam was as an animal, made from the earth, when God picked him up[7] and breathed Holy Spirit into him. Immediately, a separation occurred between mankind and all the animals. Unlike any other living creature, Adam now possessed what some scholars call the majestic nature of God. Adam's soul and spirit were indistinguishable, and they totally controlled the actions of his body in doing the work that God told him to do.

God's voice was heard by Adam's spirit as he humbled himself before his Master, which was in turn passed to his soul which resulted in obedience. This is the proper government of the trinity of a person. This is God's original intent with the spirit, under God's direction, superseding and leading the soul and body.

Mankind is Broken at the Fall:

> *And they heard the voice of the LORD God walking in the garden in the cool of the day: and Adam and his wife hid themselves from the presence of the LORD God amongst the trees of the garden.*
>
> — GENESIS 3:8

The fall of man in the Garden of Eden totally changed everything. Mankind fled and hid from the presence of God. This led to the separation of man's living soul from God's Spirit and resulted in a broken race of beings. The nature of man went from the reflection of the majestic nature of God's likeness and image to that of animals who by nature are instinctual and bestial.

> *And GOD saw that the wickedness of man was great in the earth, and that every imagination of the thoughts of his heart was only evil continually.*

— GENESIS 6:5

Without the influence of God's breath, or Holy Spirit, man began to follow the voice of the lusts and appetites of the flesh. This became progressively more wicked and evil over the generations. No longer did mankind have access to the thoughts and voice of God, and he had grown to the fullest state of what the Bible calls a reprobate mind. Mankind became a creature in desperate straits who was without the peace that only comes from being in relationship with God.

Lack of Proper Government = Listening to Wrong Voices

The carnality, or worldliness, of the fallen nature is the fruit of a person whose spirit is dead to the things of God. I have already mentioned the overemphasis that the unsaved and baby Christians tend to place upon the voice of the flesh which speaks through their lusts and appetites. On the other hand, the soul, or mind, receives input from the voice of the five senses, which also impacts decision making. Meanwhile, the voice of a man's spirit is largely ignored and remains underdeveloped. As a result, the personal government of unsaved man is the authority exercised by the evil thoughts and imaginations in the soul and it is supplemented by the animalistic nature in the body. As one would expect, the words that heathen speak reflect this.

Who is in charge in the unbeliever's life? The individual person is. This is the legacy of fallen man!

. . .

Reconciliation

> *For the Son of man is come to seek and to save that which was lost.*
>
> — LUKE 19:10

In God's perfect timing, He sent Jesus Christ His Son to restore us back to God's original intent. Jesus died on the cross for our sins and totally paid the necessary redemptive price. By making Jesus Savior and Lord in faith, we are born again.

The heart of Father God is for all men to be saved and be restored back to the original intent. He initiates this through the preaching of the Gospel which is the seed. The ministry of Holy Spirit acts upon this seed in order to draw our hearts to repentance and salvation. Everyone must decide, "Who do you say that Jesus is?" It is a choice we all must make![8]

If we resist this call of conviction on our hearts, we will never get out of the starting gate to fulfilling our destiny. The government of our life will remain under the control of evil thoughts and lusts of the flesh. As a result, the proper cultivation of the other fields will be nothing more than foolishness to us. This is the authority of the unsaved or carnal mind. This is fed by what we see in the natural world and leads to death.

> *No man can come to me, except the Father which hath sent me draw him: and I will raise him up at the last day.*
>
> — JOHN 6:44

No one can just decide at random to get right with God of

His own volition. Holy Spirit begins the work of salvation by gently pulling on the heart by convicting us of our sins, which need to be repented of. We must be born again, a spiritual event preceded by the mental persuasion resulting from the foolishness of preaching. We must also believe that God raised Him from the dead. Also, we must confess with our mouth, as we speak from the heart, that Jesus Christ is Lord and Master of our life. We are to speak our salvation into being through this confession. Remember, the power of life and death are in the tongue.[9]

Each of us must decide whether to receive Jesus as the Master and Lord of our life. This is accomplished by childlike faith. As a result, the government of our spirit, soul, and body is restored to God's original intent. We are now restored to the ability of hearing and of responding to God's voice.

Remember that there is an altar before the throne of God. This implies a sacrifice is expected for those who approach His presence. What do we sacrifice on the altar as we approach His throne when we are born again? We surrender our life to Him for His purposes. This is not to obtain fire insurance that keeps us out of hell.

> *But ye shall receive power, after that the Holy Ghost is come upon you: and ye shall be witnesses unto me both in Jerusalem, and in all Judaea, and in Samaria, and unto the uttermost part of the earth.*
>
> — ACTS 1:8

Another decision after being born again is whether to receive the baptism of Holy Spirit with the evidence of speaking in tongues. The baptism of Holy Spirit does not make us any better as a Christian than others, but it does makes us better equipped for God's use than we would be otherwise.

He brings to us the power and strength required to increase the Kingdom of God. In the author's opinion, the baptism of Holy Spirit is the full restoration of the individual's ability to accomplish his God-ordained purpose.

First Aspect of Field #1: Proper Government Within Ourselves

> *And the very God of peace sanctify you wholly;*
> *and I pray God your whole spirit and soul*
> *and body be preserved blameless unto the*
> *coming of our Lord Jesus Christ.*
>
> — 1 THESSALONIANS 5:23

Today, we can be restored to proper relationship with God through salvation by faith in Jesus Christ. When we are born again, our spirit is awakened to fellowship with God's Holy Spirit. Holy Spirit is our teacher and comforter and speaks to us what Father God wants us to hear and to know. Additionally, when we receive the baptism of Holy Spirit, He equips us with the power to accomplish our purpose for being born, to be His witnesses in expanding the Kingdom of God.[10]

Second Aspect of Field #1: The Discipline of Waiting Upon the Lord

The born again Christian has regained access, through the

blood sacrifice of Jesus Christ, to the presence and voice of God. We are called to wait upon the Lord. Remember, disciples practice discipline. The daily discipline of waiting upon the Lord is the practical application of BARAK in our lives. Please refer to the section in chapter 4 that gives detailed suggestions on how to establish this daily discipline in your life.[11]

When we are born again, we become a new spiritual creature. The baptism of Holy Spirit equips us to go into darkness to witness the gospel of the Kingdom of God. However, there is still the matter of our soul, or mind, the seat of our intellect. This part of our being has not been changed. It is still corrupted with the thoughts of violence, evil, and wickedness that is in the world. This must be dealt with, or our souls will not be in unity with the voice which our spirit hears as God speaks to us. As a result, we may find ourselves resisting the will of God. This must be properly dealt with by the process of renewing our mind.

What do we sacrifice on the altar before God's throne when we wait on the Lord? We give up some of our time, energy, and perhaps our hobbies or other interests as we practice the discipline of waiting upon the Lord.

Third Aspect of Field #1: The Daily Discipline of Renewing Your Mind

> *I beseech you therefore, brothers, by the mercies of God, that you present your bodies a living sacrifice, holy, acceptable unto God, which is your reasonable service. And be not conformed to this world: but be transformed by the renewing of your mind, that ye may*

> *prove what is that good, and acceptable, and perfect, will of God.*
>
> — ROMANS 12:1-2

Our souls must be transformed by His Word, to His thoughts. This is done by the renewing of our mind through the disciplined reading and meditation of His Word. The Greek word translated "transformed" is METAMORPHOO, from which we get the word metamorphosis. This word draws a mental picture of the change that a caterpillar undergoes in becoming a butterfly. When we renew our mind, our spirit and soul come into unity to what He has spoken or shown us in our spirit. Our born again spirit already bears witness with His word, but our mind must be trained to discern the things of the Kingdom. When our soul and spirit come into unity, the body has no choice but to line up in action. This is what happens when we fashion ourselves to align with God's mind and character.[12]

> *... when thou shalt make his soul an offering for sin, he shall see his seed, he shall prolong his days, and the pleasure of the LORD shall prosper in his hand. He shall see of the travail of his soul, and shall be satisfied: by his knowledge shall my righteous servant justify many...*
>
> — ISAIAH 53:10-11

Jesus gave us an example to follow by the way He sacrificed His soul for each of us. He willingly laid down His ambitions, feelings, emotions, and ultimately, His life as a sacrifice on the altar before the throne of God. The Hebrew word NEPESH is translated as soul and refers to the inner man or soul of a person. This deals specifically with the appetites, emotions, passions, will, and character in our lives.[13]

Practical Application of Renewing Our Mind

How do we go about the discipline of renewing our mind?

1. Settle in your mind that the Word of God is absolutely true, and will deliver us from our afflictions. (Psalm 119:89-92).
2. God blesses us and makes us whole when we live our life according to His Word (Psalm 1:1).
3. When we hide His Word in our heart, we will be kept from committing sin (Psalm 119:11).
4. Read the Word out loud to yourself. Speak it daily as a part of your life. (Psalm 119:13).
5. Meditate on the scriptures. The word meditate is not to be interpreted from a new age religious perspective, but rather it means to chew over and over like a cow chews his cud (Palms 119:15).
6. Meditate by memorizing the scriptures. Set goals of how many you wish to memorize in a set period of time. Place copies at strategic places you frequent daily such as on your refrigerator, on the vanity mirror in your bathroom, on the dashboard in your car, etc. Read, memorize, and quote out loud every time you see it.
7. Meditate by visualizing how the scripture can be applied in a practical way in your life.

8. Meditate by personalizing the scripture. Make the quality decision that the principles that you have learned in this process will dictate how you will act from now on.
9. Make this discipline of renewing of your mind a delight in your life. The word delight means to make this your priority, business, pursuit, pleasure, and the necessity of your life. This discipline is of great value for you to pursue.

Fourth Aspect of Field #1: The Discipline of Speaking Properly

> *A man's belly shall be satisfied with the fruit of his mouth; and with the increase of his lips shall he be filled. Death and life* are *in the power of the tongue: and they that love it shall eat the fruit thereof.*
>
> — PROVERBS 18:20-21

Whatever voice governs the soul is reflected in the words that come out of one's mouth. This is a heart issue. Out of the heart or soul the mouth speaks. This defines not only how we speak, but who or what we worship and serve. Generally, you can usually tell within a few minutes of conversation what a person believes in, and what they serve.

It is vitally important to understand that the power of life and death is in the words we speak. How powerful are words? The universe itself was created and is held together by the words spoken by the Messiah. Jesus made the way for us to be like Him. Speaking properly is our choice!

Remember, that in Genesis 1 God spoke creation, which was good, into existence. This is a biblical pattern for us to follow. When we read His Word and have renewed our minds, Holy Spirit will often lead us to pray by reading or quoting scripture from memory. These words still retain as much power and authority today as they did the moment they were originally spoken by Him. When we speak, decree, or declare according to His Word, we bring forth good as we experience "on earth as it is in heaven."

> *But what saith it? The word is nigh thee, even in thy mouth, and in thy heart: that is, the word of faith, which we preach; That if thou shalt confess with thy mouth the Lord Jesus, and shalt believe in thine heart that God hath raised him from the dead, thou shalt be saved. For with the heart man believeth unto righteousness; and with the mouth confession is made unto salvation.*
>
> — ROMANS 10:8-10, KJV

What is the most important thing we speak concerning the field within ourselves? This involves a process. The Word is birthed in our hearts when we hear someone preach the message of the Gospel of the Kingdom of God. Holy Spirit then begins to germinate the seed of the Word in our heart. He stirs us and convicts us of our sins as He draws us to the Father. At that point, we all must make the choice of surrendering our life to Him or not. For those who choose to surrender, we confess with our mouth that we receive Him as Lord and Savior, and we renounce all the works of darkness and sin in our life. We repent, turn from the old life, and convert our lives totally to serve Him. This ongoing process requires both speaking and action!

Even after we are born again and have lived for God for years, we still must deal with the Adamic nature which is at work in the flesh of man. This brings unclean thoughts of violence, wickedness, evil, lusts, and appetites of the flesh. We are to hold every thought captive and bring it into order by using the standard of the Word. The mind and the thoughts of Christ are expressed to us by His Word, the Bible. Therefore, it is very important to discipline our minds. God intends for His overcomers to think victoriously as they make their stand against darkness by using His Word to speak and to live by.[14]

What do you sacrifice on the altar that is before the throne of God when you renew your mind? You sacrifice your old way of thinking and replace those thoughts with His. If we do not yield this part of our life to Him, we will experience very limited success in bearing the fruit of the Kingdom.

MEMORY SCRIPTURE

Matthew 13:37-40 He answered and said unto them, He that sows the good seed is the Son of man; The field is the world; the good seed are the children of the kingdom; but the tares are the children of the wicked one; The enemy that sows them is the devil; the harvest is the end of the world; and the reapers are the angels. As therefore the tares are gathered and burned in the fire; so shall it be at the end of this age.

QUESTIONS TO PONDER

1. Do you understand that God holds you accountable to properly cultivate the three seeds of the Kingdom of God?
2. Do you live life ordered by feeding your fleshly appetites or by the reasoning of men? Or is your life ordered by the Word of God and by listening to His voice?
3. Do you actively practice the discipline of renewing your mind?

WHAT GOD SAYS ABOUT YOU

Write your answers in a notebook.

1. Read Genesis 1:26-28; 2:15- write down the three types of seed of the Kingdom. Write down how you are doing in managing each type of seed.
2. Read Romans 12:1-3; 8:5-14; Ephesians 4:17-18, 22-24- write down aspects listed about renewing your mind.
3. Read 1 Corinthians 2:16- write down what it means to have the mind of Christ.

BECOMING WHO GOD CREATED YOU TO BE:

1. Add to your daily discipline- actively renew your mind by reading, memorizing, personalizing and applying the Word of God.

2. Discuss with your pastor or mentor the practical ways that you can renew your mind when you have an active lifestyle.
3. Continue your daily discipline of asking God's purpose for today, applying your your faith to that purpose today, become aware of opportunities to sow seed today, and to determine to never take anyone else's glory and honor.

CHAPTER NINE
THE FIELD OF OUR RELATIONSHIP WITH GOD

"Have your heart right with Christ, and He will visit you often, and so turn weekdays into Sundays, meals into sacraments, homes into temples, and earth into heaven."

— CHARLES H. SPURGEON

Master, which is the great commandment in the law?... "love the Lord your God with all your heart, and with all your soul, and with all your mind. This is the first and great commandment. And the second is like unto it, you shall love your neighbor as yourself."

— MATTHEW 22:36-39

As we continue to study how to properly manage the five fields of relationships of our life, we discover that one essential element is always involved. Love!!! We are to love God and to love our neighbors as ourselves. We have already begun to uncover this truth in the last chapter as we examined the government of our soul, or of the mind. We have learned that this is an expression of the seed of rule and is revealed through the words we speak. This starts at salvation. Everything in our spiritual walk begins with receiving Jesus as both Lord and Savior of our life, which has been made possible through the greatest act of love in history. God loved us so much that He sent His only Son to die for us on the cross, so that we may come back into the relationship He has always intended for us to have.

When we were born again, we were enabled to cross over a bridge that was previously closed to us, the bridge that leads to a relationship with God. We start across this bridge by moving away from selfishness and self-love and begin to move toward learning about the love of God in our life. We are now enabled to cross from the Field #1- The Field of Relationship within Yourself to Field #2- The Field of Relationship with God. Keep this pattern in mind as we also examine the three seeds we sow into the five fields.

As we discuss Fields #2 - #5 to help our understanding, please reference the section in the last chapter of how the three seeds and the five fields relate to our lives.

Field #2- The Field of Relationship with God: This field deals with the government of our spirit, or of how we live. Worship and praise are important in our relationship with God, and they are the type of food which feeds our spirit. Worship and praise deal with the seed of the heart, or of rule. Even as we must eat meat to stay healthy and strong in our body, so must we worship God to stay strong and healthy in our spirit! Also, the proper management of this field includes how we manage our money and resources, which is the seed of increase. As we learn to worship Him and properly manage the seed of increase, we can expect changes to occur in our life. We will increasingly become a giver, and we will no longer be driven by the sin of a selfish person who is in bondage to the lusts of the Adamic nature. God's love will begin to stir us to action!

We will now begin our discussion of three major aspects of how we cultivate our relationship with God. First, we undergo transformation through our worship. Second, we must learn to properly manage our money. Third, we need to learn how to hear God's voice.

First Aspect of Field #2: Transformation Through Worship-John 17:17-19

When we are drawn by the Spirit of God and make the decision to surrender our life to Him, we undergo the experience of being born again. All things are new and old things pass away. However, this is not the end of the matter, but only the beginning of a process called sanctification, or transformation, into the image of Christ. We are to become like Him. Our spirit becomes alive and sensitive to God, which begins the process of transformation. Our spirit is reborn and comes alive again to the things of God. As a result, we will desire to worship Him!

Man was created with a need to fellowship with, to worship, and to serve God. Please take note that God made us this way. But what if we are not a believer and do not serve God? We will find something or someone else to worship instead to meet this inherent need. Whatever it is we worship, we will also serve and honor as our master. In fact, a spiritual hunger in the spirit of every person is fed only by worshiping God. Worship of other gods never satisfies (Psalm 115:1-18)!

Although there are many Hebrew words that deal with worship and praise, seven main words in the Old Testament are the most commonly used to define how we are to worship God. None of these have been done away with in the New Testament.

The ways God desires for us to worship and praise Him are:

- Ps. 42:5- to YADA, praise in lifting our hands as in throwing rocks or shooting arrows, or as a little child reaching up to Father.
- Ps.50:23- to TOWDAH, showing agreement with the extended right hand.
- Ps 95:6- to BARAK, humbling ourselves by bowing before Him.
- Ps.22:3- to TEHILLAH, singing spontaneously.
- Ps 150- to ZAMAR, plucking the strings, to celebrating in song and in music.
- I Chron 16:4- to HALAL, being clamorously foolish by dancing, twirling, and leaping.
- Ps 63:3-4- to SHABACH, shouting, or addressing in a loud tone.

Worship and praise are how we feed our spirit-man, but as a result of the Fall in the Garden, it is not a "natural" thing for us to do. However, we are told to love God in Matthew 26:36-39, and the only way we can show love to God is to obey Him in faith. The Adamic nature is still alive in our flesh and resists the things of God, even though the Bible teaches that we are to worship Him. Some of the ways God wants us to be obedient in our worship are to wait upon the Lord, to sing, to dance, to clap, to shout, or to play an instrument. This starts in our private devotional life and progressively becomes evident as an outward expression during corporate worship. Those who do not worship God in private will not worship Him in public. This results in a testimony which speaks loudly of the level of one's relationship with Jesus, both good and bad (1 Corinthians 2:14).

> *But You* are *holy,* O You *that inhabits the praises of Israel.*
>
> — PSALM 22:3

Often, we find that as we worship God, we will hear His voice speaking to us. This really is not a surprise, as the Bible teaches that God inhabits the praises of His people. Also, as we learned in Genesis 1, the Father created us to hear His voice whenever we wait upon Him, and this is true of worship as well. Therefore, we should endeavor (Mark 4:24) to have pen and paper available whenever we worship and expect that God will often give us His marching orders as we worship. There is nothing wrong with stopping momentarily to write down what He reveals to us; otherwise, we may become distracted and forget what He has revealed.

We must be very careful of what we listen to. The human spirit is directly impacted by what we hear. When we listen to secular music and newscasts, conversations with worldly-minded friends, and to teachings of false teachers and false prophets, seeds of darkness are placed in our spirits. Beware of these counterfeits of truth which will hinder our walk with God. This is the food that feeds the spirit of the unsaved and we are called to separate ourselves from these things (2 Peter:1-3).

> *Finally, brethren, whatsoever things are true, ...*
> *honest,... just,... pure,... lovely, of good report;*
> *if there be any virtue, and... any praise,*
> *think on these things.*
>
> — PHILIPPIANS 4:8

On the other hand, if we listen to teachings, music, and conversation that are Kingdom-oriented, seeds of light impact our spirit and soul. It is important to remember that whatever we see and hear will eventually result in action in the body.

Whatever governs your spirit man determines how you will live. If you worship and serve God as Master, your nature will begin to change to become a person who lives life as a worshipper of God. On the other hand, if you worship yourself, by default you serve Satan as your master and you will selfishly live pursuing the lusts and appetites of the flesh.

SECOND ASPECT OF FIELD #2: MANAGING THE SEED OF INCREASE

As previously mentioned, the seed of increase, or production, deals directly with how we manage the resources of the earth. This is often quantified in the form of money, which is nothing more than a medium of exchange recognized by people as tender for goods and services. In the Jewish mindset money is very spiritual, and literally represents the life of a person.[1]

Until recently, the study of Business and Economics was a part of the School of Religious Studies in most colleges. Today it is a part of the School of Science, which explains much of the unethical business practices that exist today. Why was it ever a part of religious studies? It takes integrity and faith to start and to successfully operate a business. When we provide goods and services, we literally create wealth out of nothing. When we sow our time, talents, gifts, and resources, we exercise faith that someone will give us money in return. As a result, when we work we "make" money. God created man to be creative, which separates us from all other creatures.

Rabbi Daniel Lapin[2] wrote that, "...humanity has unique and spiritual origins...no animals have developed or ever used a system of money. Animals merely seek sustenance, whereas humans actively create theirs... a man's active participation in creation of his wealth is a mark of his spiritual greatness.

How spiritual is money? Look to Proverbs 22:7 as we consider for a moment the lifestyle of those who live selfishly. Many people today live from paycheck to paycheck getting paid each Friday, but by Monday they have spent all their money. They spend every dime they make, regardless of whether it is $500 or $5,000 per week. But that is not all. They go into debt to purchase even more goods and services. The Bible teaches that a person who loans money becomes the master of the borrower and enslaves them until the debt is paid in full. Remember, we cannot serve more than one master (see Matthew 6:24).

As a general rule, debt is not of God!

> *The earth is the LORD'S, and the fulness thereof; the world, and they that dwell therein.*
>
> — PSALM 24:1

God created everything, and therefore He owns it all. He has placed man on earth as His steward, or manager, and He has made available all the resources we need to prosper. However, nothing is free, and He requires us to pay a price.

> ... *Return unto me, and I will return unto you, says the LORD of hosts. But you said, Wherein shall we return? Will a man rob God? Yet you have robbed me. But you say, Wherein have we robbed thee? In tithes and offerings. Ye are cursed with a curse: for you have robbed me...*
>
> — MALACHI 3:7-9

If you recall, we discussed the Law of CHERUM in chapter 6. God has set apart a portion of all we produce for Himself. This portion is called the tithe, which literally means, "a tenth part". This is not just any tenth part of our increase, but it is to be the choicest and the best set apart to worship and thank Him for His blessings. But this is not all.

The Bible teaches that there are three types of tithes that originated before the Law. We need to know and apply each of these to properly cultivate our relationship with God. In the process, God will begin to change us from being a taker to being a blessing to others.

- First tithe- originally given to the ministers for their use. Today this is most often used to pay church expenses for operations and ministries.
- Second tithe- paid to ourselves as we set aside money to pay for an annual spiritual pilgrimage.

This tithe breaks financial bondage and opens the door to financial prosperity.
- Third tithe- is a ten percent benevolence for the poor and needy. This is paid every three years and averages out to be three and one third percent per year.[3]

Between these three tithes, we should be setting aside 23 1/3% of our annual income. Then we are to add in the TERUMAH, which is the Hebrew word translated as "offering". This refers to the first-fruits offering which we should be giving as well. There are additional offerings they we may give to as well. God wants us to give as we are able and with our free will. Giving offerings should never be done through coercion or compulsion.

- TERUMAH (first fruits) offering = 2 2/3%- paid directly for support of the High Priest.
- Plus any other free will offerings which you wish to give anywhere God leads.

As you can see, we must learn to live on less income than we actually make. The author has found that it is a good rule of thumb is to strive to live on 60% or less of your income. When giving our tithes, the first 10% going to God is only paying what we owe Him. The second tithe is for strengthening our relationship with God and with our family. The third tithe is to help those in need, which begins to give God something to work with in blessing us. Finally, the TERUMAH opens the floodgates of finances.

Many of us look at this as being totally unrealistic and may still be barely making enough to support our family. If this is your situation, you need to start somewhere. I do not know anyone who thought they could afford to tithe when they first started. Today, I know many, including myself, who God has enabled to tithe and give even beyond what is mentioned here. Giving is a step of faith, trusting that God will meet your needs regardless. But what happens when we give? Is it gone forever? Can we expect anything to result from our giving?

> *Bring ye all the tithes into the storehouse, that there may be meat in mine house, and prove me now herewith, saith the LORD of hosts, if I will not open you the windows of heaven, and pour you out a blessing, that there shall not be room enough to receive it. And I will rebuke the devourer for your sakes, and he shall not destroy the fruits of your ground; neither shall your vine cast her fruit before the time in the field, saith the LORD of hosts. And all nations shall call you blessed: for ye shall be a delightsome land, saith the LORD of hosts.*
>
> — MALACHI 3:10-12

> *Be not deceived; God is not mocked: for whatever a man sows, that shall he also reap... to his flesh shall of the flesh reap corruption... sows to the Spirit shall of the Spirit reap life everlasting. And let us not be weary in well doing: for in due season we shall reap...*
>
> — GALATIANS 6:7-9

> *But he that received seed into the good ground is he that hears the word... understands... also bears fruit, and brings forth, some an hundredfold, some sixty, some thirty.*
>
> — MATTHEW 13:23

God tells us that we are required to take an action of our will:

- to give God His portion.
- to bring our seed of tithes and of offerings to the storehouse. This is not a person or institution, but rather the person who spiritually feeds and tends to us.
- to watch and see what God does in response to our giving.

What changes will we see in our life? God tells us that after we are obedient to give our tithes and offerings, He will take these actions:

- to open access to supernatural signs, wonders, and miracles.
- to allow us to visibly see His hand on our life.
- to rebuke the thief from stealing from us.
- to protect our seed so that it brings a harvest.
- to bless us so much that others will want to be blessed the same way.

What other changes can we expect? When we become a giver, our lives begin to change, as giving does more for us than for those we give to. Rabbi Daniel Lapin wrote, "they give money away because on some deep level, they recognize that doing so does more for the giver than it does to the recipient... give money away not because it is rational, but because it is right."[4]

Also, a scientific study[5] was recently published in Science Magazine. The researchers studied two groups of people who were given the task of spending a set amount of money. They could choose to spend the money on themselves, or to give it to someone else. An obvious pattern emerged from the results. Those who gave money away were happier than those who spent the money on themselves.

Giving is a lifestyle that is developed over time, and eventually leads us back to the state we were originally created to be, givers and not takers. Over the course of time, God will begin to bless our faithfulness by prospering us. The definition of prosperity is, to have enough to meet our needs plus some to help meet the needs of others, and to build the Kingdom. He will never give us more than we can faithfully manage. He promises that He will bless our faithfulness by giving us resources for our needs and for our giving.

When the government of our body, soul, and spirit is in correct order, there will be a direct reflection in how we worship God. This is directly reflected in how we handle the seed of increase, or our money and resources. Money no longer controls us, but rather we are enabled to use money as a tool which works for us. This defines how we handle money and resources.

Third Aspect Field #2: Hearing the Voice of God

God has a voice. There are many ways that God speaks, but primarily we hear Him in the form of the "still small voice" (by impressions in our heart or by thoughts He places in our mind), by dreams, by visions, by prophecy, by angels, by people, by circumstances, or by an audible voice. Sometimes He speaks through reflections in nature. Regardless of His chosen way to speak to us[6], we must carefully listen to what He says. The mind of an immature Christian is still full of wickedness and of evil imaginations of the heart. Unless our thought-life is changed through the renewing of the mind, these evil strongholds will hinder, and even resist, the voice of God.

God really wants us to know what He has to say, and He has even been known to speak through a donkey to communicate with an ungodly prophet. Also, He doesn't seem to have trouble speaking when He wants to be heard. He has even been known to speak to the unsaved, as He did with Cornelius. The issue is not about whether God speaks to His people or not, but rather are we willing to become sensitive enough to hear what He is speaking?

> *There are... many kinds of voices in the world, and none of them is without significance.*
>
> *— 1 Corinthians 14:10*

There are four main voices[7] we must deal with daily. First, the devil's voice is the accuser who brings disorder and attempts to hinder us with fear and intimidation. The devil also uses the voice of reason which brings fear. Second, the voice of the flesh condemns us by continuously recalling our bad experiences and mistakes. Third, the voice of the world systems tempts us and stirs up the lusts and appetites of the flesh. Finally, the voice of God is the voice of faith and truth.

How can we tell if the voice we hear is the voice of God? The more that we seek God and try to hear Him, the more sensitive we grow in discerning the difference between His and the other voices (John 10:27), but there are safeguards available to help with this as well.

> *Casting down imaginations, and every high thing that exalts itself against the knowledge of God, and bringing into captivity every thought to the obedience of Christ...*
>
> — 2 Corinthians 10:5

Again, how do we know if the voice we are listening to is of God or not? Whatever we hear or discern must line up exactly with what the Bible says. That is our measuring stick because God never contradicts His Word.

> *Beloved, believe not every spirit, but try the spirits whether they are of God: because many false prophets are gone out into the world. Hereby know you the Spirit of God: Every spirit that confesses that Jesus Christ is come in the flesh is of God: And every spirit that confesses not that Jesus Christ is come in the flesh is not of God...*
>
> — 1 John 4:1-3

There are other ways available by which we can discern which voice we may be hearing. Always consider the witness of Holy Spirit in our heart. If something is not right, we will feel an uneasiness in our heart from the witness of Holy Spirit. On the other hand, God's voice is always accompanied by peace. Another safeguard is wise counsel. Proverbs 24:6 reminds us it is always good to have a mature Christian to talk to just to make sure what we are hearing is of God or not. There is safety in a multitude of counsel.

Even when we have done everything we know to do to hear God, sometimes it is extremely difficult because of the challenges and cares of the world. The following true story is a good example of what we must do in such times.

Have you ever had one of those times where unforeseen circumstances come like a flood to such a point, that you just don't know what to do? I vividly remember one of those occasions when my pastor and I were praying for clear direction from God. We fasted and prayed over several days, but were still uncertain of what action to take. At times like these, the cares of life and the weightiness of circumstances may become so intense that it becomes difficult to hear God's voice. So, we decided to get away from the distractions and go to a quiet place we had gone during such times in the past.

Even though I was the principal of our school and an elder in the church, I was still very young and immature in the things of the Kingdom of God. We were a small church at the time and several of us were rushed into ministry before we were ready. However, I was about to learn a great lesson on that day which has served me well over the years. We arrived at a parking area on the shore of a large lake about 45 minutes away from our church. The head of a hiking trail started next to the parking lot. I love the outdoors and was looking forward to the hike. After about fifteen minutes, we sat down on a bench that had been installed by the side of the trail.

The weather on that day was perfect for being in the woods, and there was no one else around. As soon as we sat down, I began to pray and cry out to God. In retrospect, I now realize that I was duplicating our earlier prayers and that God had already heard our petition. After about 20 to 30 minutes of zealous prayer, I began to run out of things to pray. I expected my pastor to pray as well, but found that he continued to sit quietly. The only other thing I heard besides my voice were crickets in the background.

After a few awkward minutes, I asked my pastor if he was going to pray or not. He was an excellent mentor, and gently said, "We have come to hear what God has to say." That was it! So, I shut my mouth and began to be still, to watch, and to listen to what Holy Spirit was saying and doing.

My pastor and I waited on the Lord for two to three hours that day. When we went home, we knew exactly what we were supposed to do. Through the discipline of seeking and waiting upon the Lord, we had touched the Father's heart. He in turn spoke to both of us in such a way that we could hear exactly what His will was on the matter. We both now had the revelation that we had prayed and fasted for. We simply had to stop, to sit down, and to listen.

On a side note, we did pray together before we left for home, but it was more of a declaration of what He had spoken to us and lasted only two to three minutes. That was all that was required as we prayed the prayer of agreement exactly in line with God's perfect will. As a result, we immediately began to experience results and answers. An emergency had been turned to our good!

In this story, we had two men who sacrificed their food,

money, and time in order to hear the Master's will. This is what it takes! There are no shortcuts or freebies in the Kingdom of God. A good example for us to follow in this respect is found in 2 Samuel 24:24. King David, a man after God's own heart who never asked God for anything unless it cost him something. David was willing to pay the price, and so must we.

Practical Application of Managing the Field of Relationship with God

> *But without faith* it is *impossible to please* him:
> for he that comes to God must believe that
> He is, *and* that *He is a rewarder of them*
> that diligently seek him.
>
> — Hebrews 11:6

Believers have been created to show God honor. You do this through cultivating the fields of our relationships. So far we have discovered that cultivation begins by having a daily quiet time with God and in reading and memorizing the scriptures. Then we learned that He wants you to worship and to praise Him. As is always the case, God requires you to have child-like faith, as directed in Matthew 18:3-5.

Dr. Mack Ballard has provided this simple model to follow of how we exercise child-like faith in daily living. This simplifies how you daily deal with the field of our relationship with God in worship, in giving, and in hearing His voice.

Daily Discipline- there are four things we need to do daily:

1. Have faith in God for one day at a time, just for

today. Psalm 11:1- "Now faith is", faith that is exercised at this moment of time which is called now. It is not for the past or for the future, it is for right now. We are to apply only the faith required for what God is speaking for us to today. I daily ask, "God, what is on Your heart today, what is Your purpose today?"

2. <u>Surrender daily to God's "today" plans.</u> Do not worry about tomorrow! I daily ask, "God, what do You want me to do to help fulfill Your purpose for my life today." Worship is often integrated with my prayer. After He speaks, I apply my faith to walk it out.

3. <u>Plant seeds in good ground daily.</u> Continuously look for opportunities, as well as listen for Holy Spirit direction, of where to sow your time, money, and talents to those in need. Sow the seed of rule, or words of life, as you share your testimony, pray for, or encourage those you encounter daily. Everyday there is at least someone God brings across my path to sow into! Often, there are several.

4. <u>Never be a glory robber.</u> Always give God the glory for everything. Look for those who deserve honor and give them the honor they deserve. Never take someone else's glory for yourself.

If you will daily apply these four things, I believe God will see you as a faithful vessel of His love. The author has found that after you become faithful in diligently doing these things, God begins to bring more people to you than ever before. You will have an increased awareness that you have something to give which others greatly desire. Often, they are in desperate straits. He rewards those who He knows will be faithful to sow His Kingdom into the lives of others.

After a person has been born again and confesses Jesus as Lord and Savior, the bridge to relationship with God opens up. This is Field #2 where you learn how to worship and praise God and to become a giver rather than a taker. Also, you learn to listen and to discern His voice in this field. As a result, a second bridge opens for you which leads to the Field #3, the field of our relationship with family which we discuss in the next chapter. What we learn and apply in Field #1, the field within yourself, and in Field #2, the field of relationship with God, enables us to be successful in Fields #3- #5, the fields of relationship with your family, your church, and the world.

MEMORY SCRIPTURE

Deuteronomy 6:13-14 Thou shalt fear the LORD thy God, and serve him, and shalt swear by his name. Ye shall not go after other gods, of the gods of the people which are round about you;

QUESTIONS TO PONDER

1. What does God say about your discipline of worship and praise?
2. What does God say about your discipline of giving?
3. What does God say about your discipline of hearing the voice of God and obeying?

WHAT GOD SAYS ABOUT YOU

Write your answer in a notebook.

1. Read Psalm 22:3, 42:5, 50:33, 63:3-4, 95:6; Psalm 150; 1 Chronicles 16:4- Reread the section in this chapter about worship. List the seven ways God has defined for us to worship Him.
2. Read Malachi 1:7-8; 3:7-12- write down the problems and solutions given for tithes and offerings. List the results of giving properly.
3. Read 1 Corinthians 14:10; 2 Corinthians 10:5; I John 4:1-3; 1 Samuel 15:22- write down God's perspective of His will for you in listening to His voice and in the necessity of recognizing it from the other voices.

BECOMING WHO GOD CREATED YOU TO BE

1. Add to your daily discipline- begin to incorporate into your devotional time each of the seven different ways to worship. What you do in private overflows into corporate worship.
2. Meet with your pastor or mentor to discuss how to become a better giver. Ask them about the difference between your seed and your bread.
3. Set a goal to become more sensitive to discerning God's voice. Ask your pastor or mentor what they do in their own life to become more sensitive.

Chapter Ten
The Field of Our Relationship with Family

You can always tell how a man is doing in his relationship with God by how he treats his wife.

— -Dr. Benny Charles Hand

> *And the LORD God took the man, and put him into the garden of Eden to dress it and to keep it... and the LORD God said, "It is not good that the man should be alone; I will make him an help meet for him."*
>
> — Genesis 2:15, 18

Immediately when the family walked into my office, I realized they were going to be a good fit. They had just moved into town and were considering enrolling their children in our Christian school. Indeed, they immediately enrolled their kids and prospered in our program for several years. The father was a brilliant man, one of only a handful of specialists in the world who worked as an engineer in nuclear power plants. There was one such plant in our general area about an hour's drive away. The family was given the impression that he would be permanently stationed there, even though the company had contracts to service nuclear power plants throughout the nation.

Over the course of time, the family became settled. Our area was their new home! Everything seemed to be going well until the company called and needed the father's services elsewhere. They offered him a substantial raise to move and work in a nuclear power plant in another area of the country. This presented a dilemma! The family wanted to stay in the area since they loved their church, school, and community. However, everyone knew dad had to work. So, the family made the decision that dad would commute weekly to the other plant, which was 10 hours away. He would live in an apartment there during the week and planned to commute home on the weekends.

Now, let's pause in this story for a moment to consider what was happening. This man was a good man, a hard worker, and a good provider for his family. His demeanor was such that everyone knew he was not afraid to step up and protect his wife and kids as needed. Also, he was a believer who led the family in daily prayer and took them to church every week. In other words, he was faithful in being the provider, protector, and priest for his family. These are the three aspects of sacrifice and service that a man of God does for his family, as we shall see later in this chapter. However, he was about to make a major mistake by removing himself from the home and felt that he was "meeting his obligation" to them by making more money. However, there were unexpected consequences from removing himself from the daily influence he had on the family.

To make a long story short, the kids missed their dad's influence, and the mom, was stretched thin in managing the household by herself. As principal of the school, I was with the kids daily and did everything I could to be a surrogate father for them. However, this was not the same as the dad being home. After several months, the kids began to struggle and the mom began to burn out from being overloaded.

One day, the father gave me a call. He was at a loss and was seeking advice on what to do in this situation. Honestly, he felt that he was fulfilling his responsibility by providing well for his family. It became apparent in our conversation that he was blind to the needs of the family for his presence, protection, and discipline, as well as spiritual leadership. However, he realized his wife could not handle everything by herself and was under tremendous stress as a result.

My counsel was that he needed to get the family together under one roof as soon as possible. God's plan was not only for a husband to provide for the family's needs, but also to co-labor with his wife in raising the kids. This is not accomplished in long distance relationships. Also, he needed to recognize the necessity of his role as protector and as priest in bringing stability to the home. He listened quietly and said he would pray about it.

As a result, at the end of the school term the family relocated to the community where the dad was working. This was a mixed blessing for me in that I knew they were doing the right thing, but I also knew I was going to miss them. However, we always need to do the right thing.

Over the course of time, I received another phone call from the dad who called to thank me for the advice. He shared about how well the family was doing and how he had learned a great lesson in this process. Indeed, there is no substitute for having our family in proper biblical order. Let's now consider aspects of our relationship with our family as we continue our study of yield to yield.

Field #3-The Field of Relationship with Family: This field deals with the institution of marriage, with raising children, and with learning how to relate to other people. This focuses primarily on management of the seed of the body. As Christians, we are to have a multi-generational perspective and to declare God's vision to all generations. As a result, the sacrifices we are called to make are for multiple generations, not just our own.

Please consider that we are living simultaneously in all five fields of relationships. Growth should be progressive in each field and will have a ripple effect upon the other fields, which allows for an increased capacity to grow in the others as well. Even as a child goes through different stages of growth from being a newborn baby to becoming a fully mature adult, so it is with our spiritual growth in each field. We need to be aware that we cannot grow complacent in any area that God reveals that we need to change and to grow in. Otherwise, we will be hindered in being able to complete our mission.

Therefore, after one has been born again and has begun to be transformed by the renewing of our mind, change and growth should manifest in the other fields. We are then capable of properly worshiping God and of becoming a giver. We can then effectively manage the field of the family. This process increasingly impacts the other fields as well.

Marriage was the first institution[1] established by God. Marriage is defined in the Bible as a covenant relationship between a man and a woman for the purpose of building the Kingdom of God and to raise God-fearing children. Due to the decrease in the average lifespan of man, it is essential we understand that a multigenerational mindset is required to accomplish our purpose. As a general rule, whenever God gives a man a mission to accomplish, it will take several generations to accomplish it.

We will now begin our discussion of three major aspects of how we cultivate our relationship with family. First, we need to understand God's original intent for marriage. Second, we need to understand the God-ordained government which He has designed to bring proper order to the family. Third, we learn what it means to submit to one another through meeting one another's needs. These prepare us to successfully cultivate the next field, the relationship between ourselves and the church which we will discuss in chapter 11.

First Aspect of Field #3: God's Original Intent for Marriage

> *And God blessed them, and God said... Be fruitful, and multiply, and replenish the earth, and subdue it:*
>
> — Genesis 1:28

As we have previously discussed, Genesis 1:28 is one of the crucial scriptures for God's purpose in creating man. As a result, we are to seek His direction daily, then we are to act in obedience! At this point, we will consider an additional aspect of how we are equipped to accomplish our mission. We are told to be ..."fruitful and multiply...", to have children and to occupy the whole earth. As we do this, we carry the Kingdom of God with us wherever we go. Obviously, this now becomes

Woman was perfectly created to be the helpmeet[3] for her husband. This is not a term of subservience as seen in the usage of this word in several scriptures, which is used to describe God's role in His relationship with man. The mental picture drawn in the Hebrew of Eve's creation out of Adam, was that she was created from a rib located on the front of Adam's ribcage. Often, this has been interpreted as a rib on Adam's side, which could symbolize woman as being by his side in order to help him. However, I believe we may glean a much deeper meaning from this. A wife is not merely to stand at his side, but rather to be face-to-face and mouth-to-mouth with her husband. There are obvious procreation implications here, but it is much more than that. Eve was created to complete Adam in every way. As a general rule, it is not good for man to be alone.

In the analogy mentioned above, the Church as the Bride of Christ, is to be face-to-face and mouth-to-mouth with her groom, Jesus Christ!

C.S. Lewis wrote[4] about how the creation story of Adam and Eve relates to Christian marriage today, "The Christian idea of marriage is based on Christ's words that a man and wife are to be regarded as a single organism-for that is what the words one-flesh means... male and the female, were made to be combined together in pairs, not simply on the sexual level, but totally combined."

3. God's original intent of marriage was for the husband and wife to be co-equals in their relationship and in serving Him. Woman was not created to be subservient to man in any way.

There is no indication in the Genesis creation narrative

that Adam or Eve was the leader, and the other was their servant. They were created equals. This stands in stark contrast[5] to the historical patterns in which women were accorded very little freedom or dignity. For example, in pagan cultures the women were treated as chattel and the men stood superior to them. Greek women were kept under lock and key and treated essentially as a slave. Roman women had a high rate of infanticide, little education, and were given no property rights. Roman men exercised complete ownership of their wife and allowed no interaction with the husband's quests.

Judaism and Christianity stand in stark contrast to historical patterns of the treatment of women in the world. The Jewish Study Bible[6] commentary also speaks into the creation of Adam and Eve, ..."the creation of woman after the man and from part of his body need not imply the insubordination of the woman... A man wishes for his wife to be with him always."

4. God's original intent for marriage is for both spouses to treat each other with honor, dignity, and freedom.

> *Unto the woman he said... thy desire* shall be *to thy husband, and he shall rule over thee.*
>
> — GENESIS 3:16

In Genesis 3 the fall of man is described in the Garden of Eden. The serpent was cursed by God, and in turn Eve was cursed for her part in this fiasco. God always renders judgment that is totally just and appropriate for every sin that person commits. This scripture states that a woman, "will now desire her husband". At first glance one could take this to refer to the drawing of physical intimacy between man and woman. However, she was already intimately drawn to the man even before the fall. Instead, I believe this refers to the loss of the type of relationship she had with Adam up to this point in time. Her husband was the perfect man! Remember, he was created absolutely good in the image and likeness of God. The result of the fall was devastating and much was lost.

It is the author's opinion that every woman born since the Garden of Eden still has the same desires for a husband who is the perfect man. Today, there is only one way this can be fulfilled. A man and woman can be the perfect mate if they will be born again and fully embrace all aspects of Jesus' ministry of reconciliation in their life. Eve had the perfect man in every way. As a result of her rebellion, she lost this great blessing in her life but never lost the yearning that only such a man can fill. Today, a born again believer can be the perfect spouse, but this does not automatically happen. This is only accomplished by being transformed into the image of Christ, the second Adam.

5. God's original intent for marriage was perverted by the fall in the Garden of Eden. At that time, man was given responsibility to lead his wife, and she was given responsibility to follow and to submit to him.

Second Aspect of Field #3: Proper Government in the Family

According to the Bible[7], the proper government of the family is comprised of the nuclear family. This includes the leadership of a husband with the help of his wife in building a home and a family. They are to live in a lifelong covenant relationship called marriage. They are to procreate and to raise a family to replenish the earth. God places great value on human life and He expects His people to do the same. As a result, children are to be considered a precious blessing. This has always set Christians apart and squarely places us in direct opposition to the world.

Many cultures view children[8] as a throw-away commodity, as evidenced by rampant abortion, child abuse, and abandonment. Instead of throwing away children, God expects His people to view their children as of great value. As a result, God expects parents to train children in the nurture and admonition of the Lord, and to expand the Kingdom into the future. If this is not faithfully carried out, Christianity will disappear in one generation.

> *Except the LORD build the house, they labor in vain that build it: except the LORD keep the city, the watchman awakens* but *in vain*. It is *vain for you to rise up early, to sit up late, to eat the bread of sorrows:* for *so he gives his beloved sleep. Lo, children* are *an heritage of the LORD:* and *the fruit of the womb is his reward. As arrows* are *in the hand of a mighty man; so* are *children of the youth. Happy* is *the man that hath his quiver full of them: they shall not be ashamed, but they shall speak with the enemies in the gate.*
>
> — PSALM 127: 1-5

> *Blessed* is *every one that fears the LORD; that walks in his ways. For you shall eat the labor of your hands: happy will you* be, *and it shall be well with thee. Your wife* shall be *as a fruitful vine by the sides of your house: your children like olive plants round about your table. Behold, that thus shall the man be blessed that fears the LORD. The LORD shall bless thee out of Zion: and you shalt see the good of Jerusalem all the days of your life. You shall see your children's children,* and *peace upon Israel.*
>
> — PSALM 128:1-6

Psalm 127 and 128 gives us some insight into how God intends for His people to maintain a proper perspective concerning marriage and children.

1. <u>The father is to serve as the priest of the family</u>. Everything starts with our relationship with God. Our homes are to be a sanctuary from influences of the world. This includes living our lives in the fear of the Lord, with prayer and worship integrated as a major part of the household. If the dad is disobedient, it is up to the mom to see that this is done.
2. <u>The father is to be the protector of the family</u>. A good shepherd must be willing to lay down his life for his sheep[9]. This is one of the traits of a real man of God, who realizes that his wife has a need for security.

3. The father of the family is to be the main financial provider. This requires the husband to exercise discipline in order to follow God's financial management guidelines as presented in the Bible. This includes being transformed from being a taker to becoming a giver in the image of Christ.
4. The wife is to take her conjugal duties seriously. She is to stand by her husband and be a comfort and a helpmate to him. The biblical pattern in this scripture is for the wife to stay home and raise God-fearing children to become productive members of the family and of society.
5. If parents take the biblical approach to household management, and to the raising of their children, they will be greatly blessed. Please notice that the scripture does not say it will be easy! However, if we work hard and do it in the right way, we will yield great fruit of the Kingdom.

God's original intent for the role of the husband is for him to be the priest, protector, and provider for the family. The wife is to raise the children, and to be the manager of the household. Please take note that if we attempt to build our family in any way other than according to God's Word, we risk being in violation of the Law of Unity and things will not work properly. As a result of disobedience, we run the risk of becoming disillusioned, of losing sleep as we worry about kids and finances, and of our blessings being cut off.

Third Aspect of Field #3: Serve One Another

YIELD TO YIELD

> *Submitting yourselves one to another in the fear of God.*
>
> — EPHESIANS 5:21

> *Husbands, love your wives, even as Christ also loved the church, and gave himself for it;*
>
> — EPHESIANS 5:25

In Ephesians 5:21-22, the Greek word translated[10] as "submitting" is HUPOTASSO, which means to line up in military order, to align in proper rank and file, or to willingly submit yourself to someone. This is the word commonly used for voluntary submission. It is never used in the context of forced submission and has nothing to do with humiliating yourself. The application of this word in marriage is for both spouses to determine to consistently focus upon meeting the other's needs. If each spouse strives to meet the other's needs, the marital bliss that results is a good thing! This is foundational to a good marriage. What happens if this is neglected? Problems! Based upon many years of marital counseling, I have found that selfishness is nearly always at the root of marital problems.

In Ephesians 5, a husband is to submit to his wife by loving her, which is accomplished by sacrificially giving himself to his wife. How much is he to sacrifice? Everything! The Greek word for love is AGAPE, and it is the type of sacrificial love that Jesus walked in as He gave Himself for His people. The only way a husband can do this is by first surrendering everything to Christ. If a husband is unable to do this, he has some issues in his life that need to be dealt with.

The Hebrew word for serve[11] is AVODAH, which is used for service to God and to serve people. The Hebrew word for love is AHAV, which literally means, "I give". In the ancient Hebrew, this means to never take from another person. This has nothing to do with our emotions, but is strictly based upon the actions taken as expressed in our service to those we love. God wants us to love people, which is expressed through how we serve them. As we learn to serve our spouse and children, our capacity for serving those in the church and in the world increases. The family is the training ground for learning how to serve in the other fields of relationship. There is great joy in serving and blessing others.

I have learned that there are certain things that cultivate a successful marriage. Consider the following points that I have gleaned over the course of 44 years of marriage.

- Our family needs a safe, stable, and predictable home environment.
- Our marriage success is not based on how much money we make, our good looks, or how educated we are. Marriage success is directly related to how well we communicate and how much we care for our spouse.
- Our joy and blessings in life are received by showing how much we personally care, like, appreciate, and desire to meet their needs. What we sow we will reap.
- Our spouse is different from us for a good reason, to complete what is lacking in us. As we each learn to accept and embrace these differences, we will be able to accomplish things which would otherwise be impossible for us to accomplish.

- Our spouse understands how much we love by what we do. Love is action.
- Our wife shows how much she loves us by showing honor and friendship as she stands by our side. This results in a better quality of life for both.

> *Wives, submit yourselves unto your own husbands, as unto the Lord. For the husband is the head of the wife, even as Christ is the head of the Church: and he is the savior of the body. Therefore, as the Church is subject unto Christ, so let the wives be to their own husbands in everything.*
>
> — EPHESIANS 5:22-24

The wife is called to serve her husband by willfully submitting to him. This is based upon an act of her free will and is not to be forced upon her. However, this is conditional. The admonition to submit to her husband is, '...in the Lord...'. The husband's role, as covered earlier in this chapter, is to love his wife sacrificially in laying everything down in his life for her. If a husband will be faithful to do this, she will be glad to submit her life to serve him. Remember that Eve is still craving her perfect Adam who was lost at the fall. This is the restoration of her perfect man.

What if a husband is not serious about his relationship with God, or is trying to lead his wife into blatant sin? In other words, what if he is not trying to lead her, 'in the Lord"? Does she have to submit and follow even though it is biblically wrong? The Bible consistently teachers that each of us are independent agents before God. A husband does not have the right to make the decision to make his wife to be saved, or to make her sin and rebel against God. This is true as well of the wife's relationship and influence with her husband. Each spouse is personally responsible to submit themselves spiritually to the Lord. In such cases, the wife will have to make decisions on where to take a biblical stand against ungodliness in the home. If the husband refuses to take his spiritual role, the wife may have to step up and fill it herself until he is willing to take his responsibility as the priest of the family.

Summation

There are many other things that could be included in this chapter. Literally, there are libraries of books on marriage and family relationships. Please consider that the aspects of marriage we have discussed in this chapter are the foundation upon which all these were written. Therefore, we all need to endeavor to learn and apply God's original intent for marriage. This includes how we are to align our family in proper biblical government, and how we are to serve and to meet the needs of our spouse. Everything else in our marriage will be built upon this foundation. From our growth in our marriage and family relationships, we will progressively be enabled to succeed in the relationship with our church and with the world, which will be the topics of our next two chapters.

Memory Verse

Genesis 2:18 And the LORD God said, It is not good that the man should be alone; I will make him a helpmeet for him.

QUESTIONS TO PONDER

1. Do you understand that marriage is very important to God?
2. Did you know the Bible teaches that parents, not government, have the responsibility to oversee the education of their children?
3. Do you live your life faithfully in fulfilling your biblically defined responsibilities of marriage?

WHAT GOD SAYS ABOUT YOU

Write your answers in a notebook.

1. Read Genesis 2; Ecclesiastes 4:9-10. Reread this section in this chapter on God's original intent for marriage. Write down everything that Holy Spirit brings to your attention.
2. Read Deuteronomy 6:1-14- meditate especially on verse 6. Write down every point of what applies to children's education.
3. Read Ephesians 5:21-33; Proverbs 31; - write down the biblical aspect of the role of the husband and the wife in marriage.

BECOMING WHO GOD CREATED YOU TO BE

1. Repent of selfishness and bitterness in your marriage relationship.

2. Go with your spouse to receive marital counseling from your pastor if you need help.
3. Confess daily that you are commissioned by God to serve and to meet the needs of your spouse.

Chapter Eleven
The Field of Our Relationship with the Church

"Ultimately what concerned Jesus was not the size of the crowd, it was the level of commitment."[1]

— Kyle Idelman

To the general assembly and Church of the first-born, which are written in heaven...

— Hebrews 12:23

My pastors had just volunteered to spend the next two days filling in for me on my job for free! Who had ever heard of such a thing? I had scheduled eye surgery for the next day, and the doctor told me to expect to be out of commission for a couple of days in order to give time for the healing to begin. I had taken the issue of coverage for the business to the Lord in prayer, and His answer came quickly and from a totally unexpected source. I had been in

Churches most of my life and had never seen a pastor do such a thing for a member of his church.

At that time, I was self-employed in an interior plant leasing and maintenance business. We specialized in installation and maintenance of indoor living plants in banks, restaurants, shopping malls and businesses, as well as in some homes. The plant material required consistent care, and most accounts were visited twice a week. Obviously, the surgery was presenting a scheduling problem, literally taking three days out of the middle of my work week. So, I needed help. My pastors had gone with me several times for fellowship as I serviced my accounts, so they knew what to do.

The surgery went very well, my eyes healed up nicely, and the accounts were serviced by my pastors. This was a major blessing!

Covenant Relationship

Why did my pastors help me in this way with my business? What made our Church so different? The answer is referred to biblically as covenant relationship, which was being demonstrated by the action of my pastors with a covenant brother. Covenant relationship in the Church is based upon making a priority of developing relationships first, then allowing ministry to flow forth as a result! This stands in stark contrast with the approach of the ministries in the Western Churches I had attended, which focused primarily upon ministry, numbers of attendees, and finances from which relationships would develop. These two approaches stand in direct opposition to one another.

What is Jesus' example[2], and what did He do? Jesus first developed covenant relationship with His disciples as they spent three years together. Eventually these men and women preached the Gospel of the Kingdom throughout the known world. Relationship came first, then ministry developed. This is the biblical pattern. As a result of following this biblical model, covenant relationship has always been the priority of our Church, from which all ministries flow. We have committed ourselves to a lifelong relationship with each other as members of the Church. This decision included our willingness to serve one another in the love of Jesus, a love that demands action rather than shallow emotional response.

The Hebrew[3] word BERYITH and the Greek word DIATHEKE are translated as the English word "covenant". BERYITH, which means to cut, refers to a sacred lifelong agreement between two or more men, or between God and man. This is sealed with blood. Each side enters into the agreement with the expectation that both parties are to meet certain conditions. If these are not met, the covenant is voided.

The Greek word DIATHEKE refers[4] to a will or testament. This gives an inheritance to someone if they so choose to receive it. The terms and conditions are defined strictly by God and are not based upon man's attempts to bargain the terms of the agreement.

The word covenant is used more than two hundred times in the Bible and is the word that defines the relationship between God and man. There are other covenants as well. These include the covenant of marriage between a husband and wife. For those who join a church, there should be a covenant made between the pastor and each of his members. Covenants are also made in business and are legally binding transactions. A covenant is a sacred agreement and a penalty is paid by those who break it. Covenants are ratified by oaths, by feasting, by raising monuments, by blood, by raising hands, or by plucking off shoes. Also, covenants are sealed by blood, or by passing between two pieces of meat.

In the New Covenant, we experience relationship with God through the provision of the blood of Jesus. This is nonnegotiable! Either we are covered by the blood of Christ and have relationship with God, or we are not covered by the blood and have no relationship. On the other hand, the covenant of marriage is sealed by the blood, which is released as the marriage is consummated during the intimacy experienced on the wedding night. Also, those who are committed to a church for life consistently seal their covenant by regularly cutting meat as they eat together.

Field #4-The Field of Relationship with the Church

This field deals with the government of belonging to a community of believers and how we are created to actively serve in the local Church. Through our progressive obedience and growth in the first three fields, we become enabled to serve God and other people. This is what the Church does!

The proper government in this field includes separation from ungodly fellowship in becoming a member of the community of believers, which is called the Church.

There are four major aspects of how we should cultivate the relationship we have with the Church. First, God has a very specific church that He has ordained for each of us to join. Second, we should expect certain things of the church God sets us in. Third, certain things should biblically be provided for us by the local church. The fourth aspect is that each of us has a job to do in the local church.

First Aspect of Field #4: God Sets us in a Church of His Choosing

> *Depart you, depart you, go you out from there, touch no unclean thing; go you out of the middle of her; be you clean, that bear the vessels of the LORD.*
>
> — Isaiah 52:11

> *Flee out of the middle of Babylon* [a sinful nation], *and deliver every man his soul: be not cut off in her iniquity...*
>
> — Jeremiah 51:6

God has made it very plain throughout the Bible that His people are to separate themselves from the world systems where Satan exercises influence over fallen mankind. This is still true today for born again believers. In fact, we are not only called to come out of the world, but we are also called to join a community of believers which is called the Church. The Church is a physical gathering of believers together.

> *Now you are the Body of Christ, and members in particular. But, now has God set the members every one of them in the Body, as it has pleased Him.*
>
> — I Corinthians 12:27,18

Contrary to the common usage[5] of this word today, the word church is not used biblically as a reference to a building, a meeting hall, or a denomination. Rather, it refers to a gathering of members of the Body of Christ. The focus of this gathering is not on where the group meets, which can be in a field, an arbor, a home, a coliseum, etc., but rather upon the people themselves.

If you are a Christian, are you currently a member of a local Church? Do you attend on a regular, consistent basis? Are you being taught the Word of God and are you growing in your faith? Are you in the Church because it is where you grew up, or is good for business, or is it where you have heard the voice of God speak that this is where He wants you to be?

Every believer is commanded to be an active member of a local church with whom we physically meet with on a regular basis. This raises the question of which church should we join and attend? God is not a God of confusion or of chance. We already have discussed at length the necessity of seeking His face and of listening to his voice. God wants us to seek His face for every issue we deal with. This is especially true of something that is this important. God knows that it is vital for us to be at the right place, at the right time, and with the right people to serve Him. Therefore, "God sets members" in a particular church Body. How do we know where to go? Ask Him where He wants you to be planted, and He will speak to you.

We need to hear His voice and be in the Church that He directs us to join and to regularly attend! He will put us where we can be spiritually fed and tended to, as well as a place where our gifts and talents are needed to meet the needs of others. Without our obedience, that church will be incomplete and hindered in accomplishing its mission. Each of us has a valuable role to play!

In writing this book, I have endeavored to share what I have personally known and walked in over the years. This is true of the Church we have been set in. After my wife and I were married, we began to visit churches in our community. After visiting several, we felt comfortable with the people and the pastor of a specific church. So, we had a family meeting, took a vote, and decided to join. This was a big mainline denominational church with a beautiful building which offered meetings and amenities that were very attractive. Plus, it was within walking distance of our house. In other words, this Church appealed very well to us. We did not know anything about listening for God's voice in those days. Even though this was not a Church based upon covenant relationships, God used this ministry to teach us many things in the Word of God.

After a couple of years of regular attendance at this church, God began to draw us into a deeper walk and as a result, we received the baptism in the Holy Spirit. We began to pray, and God spoke very clearly that it was time to leave and showed us where He wanted us to go. There was a new church starting in town with a handful of people who were meeting in the aerobics room of a local health spa. The room was not well maintained, but there were a few folding chairs and a podium which was available to the group. There was no access to electricity, which meant that there was no choir or sound system. In other words, there was nothing in the natural that made sense for us to move from the church we were attending. But we had a word from God! God requires His people to take a step of faith whenever we obey His voice.

As things turned out, God was putting us with a group of spiritually hungry young couples who were experiencing revival. Within a few months, the church grew to over 100 people, and we began to look for a larger meeting room. We moved three times in the first eighteen months as we continued to outgrow our facilities. More than three decades later the church is still vibrant and growing, and my wife and I are still members. God set us exactly where we were supposed to be, we entered covenant relationship with our pastor, and as a result have never seriously considered going anywhere else!

The Greek word translated as "set" in I Corinthians 12:18 is TITHEMI, which means to place, arrange, or to position. This "setting" is according to His overall plan and design, and is not to be based upon us shopping around to find the perfect church. If we will seek God's face and wait upon Him, God will speak to us exactly where He wants to set us. It is critically important that we remain open to where He wants us to be planted! We discovered through personal experience that it may not make common sense or appeal to our personal tastes.[6]

SECOND ASPECT OF FIELD #4: WHAT WE SHOULD EXPECT OF THE CHURCH

> *... that you may know how you ought to behave yourself in the house of God, which is the church of the living God, the pillar and ground of the truth.*
>
> *— I TIMOTHY 3:15*

The Greek word EKKLESIA is translated[7] as Church in the Bible. This word conveys the idea of removing oneself from something in an act of separation to something else. This is in response to a call to believers by Holy Spirit for us to separate from the world. From the growth we undergo by properly cultivating the first three fields of relationships, we will no longer live in the idolatry of unsaved people who are around us. In fact, we will find that we stand in direct opposition to how they live. Not only are we called to come out, but we are called to come in, or to gather, with His people in forming a Christian community, which is called the Church.

The author has observed a pattern[8] concerning those who have recently been born again and are earnestly seeking God. The old friends and acquaintances who we were in sin with, tend to withdraw and separate from relationship with us. This can be traumatic if we do not understand that the anointing of Holy Spirit on our lives brings conviction to sinners. This anointing will either draw people to a place of repentance, or to a place of removing themselves from our fellowship. As a result, we will need to replace these relationships, and the best place to do this is in the local church.

We can glean some very important insight into what the Church really is from the ancient Greek usage[9] of the word EKKLESIA. This describes those who were called to a prestigious assembly, made up of a group of prestigious landowners in Athens, Greece. This group met regularly as a governing body who handled the governmental business of the local community. In contrast, the national government handled the civil business of governing the nation. These two governmental bodies were separate in function and design, and they had different responsibilities. There was no conflict between them since their areas of responsibility and authority were well defined. The separation of church and state is still supposed to be true today as well.

In applying the word EKKLESIA to the Church today, Holy Spirit is calling His people in every city to gather on a regular basis for the purpose of going about the business of the

Kingdom of God. The original purpose of the Church was not to be hidden or to be obscure, as we read in Matthew 5:14, but rather to be a voice of influence and authority to the community. We are not to hide and cower in fear of persecution from the government or of religious institutions. Instead, we are called to exercise spiritual authority and to become a spiritual force to be reckoned with. This is done despite the resistance! The Church is like a city set upon the hill for all to see, or like the beacon of light piercing the darkness of the city.

According to the biblical pattern in the New Testament, initially there was one EKKLESIA in each city which met in a home, outdoors, or in a building. Each EKKLESIA was assigned by God to a specific geographical area and given responsibility for the people who lived there. In lieu of the Church being made up of a group of people, it is clear God never intended for a single person to stand alone in accomplishing this mission. It takes a team!

The Church should be a community of growing and maturing believers who have more than enough power and authority to turn the world system upside down. We should expect our influence in our community of the Kingdom of God to increase as a direct result of our efforts. However, there is a historical pattern of persecution which arises in response to this influence. The Church provides us help in such times as we stand together, instead of by ourselves, against persecution when it arises.

God's original intent was for mankind to spread His Kingdom into the darkness. His original intent today is fulfilled by us individually and as a team member of the local Church! We are to stand individually and corporately in direct opposition to the evil and corruption in civil government and religious systems. The Church is to be the salt that keeps the culture from becoming rotten, and the little bit of leaven of righteousness which leavens the whole lump of a nation.

Third Aspect of Field #4: What Should We do as a Member of the Church

> *But seek you first the Kingdom of God, and His righteousness...*
>
> — Mathew 6:33

In Matthew 6, we are called to influence with the principles[10] of the Kingdom of God the cultural systems of education, government, finance, media, arts, etc., which are in our community. This commission is reiterated in Mark 16:15-20, where we are called to go to the "KOSMOS" and preach the Word. This influence is to be accompanied by signs, wonders, and miracles which authenticate God's handiwork. The word KOSMOS refers to all the established systems of order in the world which are under the influence of Satan.

The second set of instructions[11] are given to us to carry the good news of the Gospel of the Kingdom of God to influence individuals who live in darkness. God would have all men to be saved; therefore, we are to go to every ETHNOS, which is every ethnic, racial and culture group. We are to achieve this mission when we are activated by the love and compassion of God Himself. This commission is given to us in Mathew 28:19-20 where we are instructed to teach and to make disciples. This says nothing about making converts!

- Act 2:42-43 And they continued in the Apostle's

doctrine and fellowship, and in breaking of bread, and in prayers.... And fear came upon every soul: and many wonders and signs were done by the Apostles.
- Act 2:44-45 And all that believed were together, and had all things common; and sold their possessions and goods, and parted them to all *men,* as every man had need.
- Act 2:46 And they continued daily with one accord in the temple, and breaking bread from house to house, did eat their meat with gladness and singleness of heart, praising God,... and had favor with all the people. And the Lord added to the church daily such as should be saved.

The Bible surprisingly gives very little detail as to what the Church is supposed to look like when we meet. However, we are given a model in Acts 2 of what the Church did when it was birthed in the first century. We should endeavor to do the same things today.

1. <u>*The first aspect of the Acts 2 Model is that the Bible should be taught to us regularly*</u> by a leader, or perhaps one of the other members, of the church. The Lord has gifted certain members in the body with the five-fold ministry gifts of apostle, prophet, evangelist, pastor or teacher. These individuals are supernaturally gifted to help the members to mature, to teach how to serve in the church and in the world, to spiritually build up each of the members, to help everyone come into unity, and to enable everyone to grow into a fully mature Christian. Please

be aware that the five-fold ministry gifts are not allowed to function in every church.

We should make every effort to attend a church where we can be fed with the Word of God. This may include mature Christians discipling young believers, home group meetings, Christian schools for the children, and/or Bible College. Whatever format is used, we all need to be fed the Word of God to grow!

2. *The second aspect of what the Church does in the Acts 2 Model is to provide for our need for fellowship with other believers.* This may be the most important thing that the Church provides. After all, we can study the word, pray, and worship individually at home. However, it is often hard for us to get the fellowship we need in the marketplace or at our job. This was especially true during the first century as persecution caused many to be totally ostracized by their community. The only place they found for belonging and for fellowship was in the Church.

Today, we find there is still a need for a venue for good Christian fellowship. Our fast-paced culture causes many people to be lonely with few friends and with no one they can depend on. Many people do not even know the names of their neighbors. The Church brings this stability back into the lives of people.

3. *The third aspect of the what the Church does in the Acts 2 Model is to regularly break bread together.* It has been said that the people who pray together stay together. This may be true to a degree, but too many church splits testify that this is not the case. However, the people who eat together do stay together. Eating is an aspect of covenant relationship that breaks down walls and brings people closer together. Consider for a moment what

happens when we sit down to eat with someone we do not really know. After the initial awkwardness, we become increasingly more comfortable with them as we eat. The conversation tends to grow in depth as we spend time over the meal. This spiritual dynamic removes walls of isolation, insecurity, and loneliness.

The church we attend should regularly promote events which include eating a meal, or at least snacks, together. Some churches I know eat after church every Sunday! Also, the individual members should be encouraged to eat meals with one another on a regular basis. Home group meetings are great for this. Unity results in a church who eats together!

4. *The fourth aspect of the what the Church does in the Acts 2 Model is to pray together in corporate prayer.*

James 5:16 is the basis for this aspect. The spiritual authority of the prayer of one righteous person can avail much. However, when praying with two or more people in agreement, there is an exponential increase in the authority and power exercised in the prayer of agreement.

> *Therefore confess your sins to each other and pray for each other so that you may be healed. The prayer of a righteous person is powerful and effective.*
>
> — JAMES 5:16 NIV

The discipline of prayer seen in Matthew 16:17-19 brings a military aspect to the church's role in our community. God has given us the authority to bind demonic strongholds and entities who have spiritual authority over our city. It is the local EKLLESIA's responsibility through prayer to "man the gates" of the city and to shift the influence from darkness and evil to a manifestation of "on earth as it is in heaven".

5. *The fifth aspect of what the Church does in the Acts 2 model is to praise and worship God together.* This is to be done with voices and/or instruments, with hymns, with songs, and with spiritual songs. Ephesians 5:19 - Every one of us should come to the assembly prepared to praise and worship God. He inhabits the praises of His people, and our corporate worship can help to bring His manifest presence.

6. *The sixth aspect of what the Church does in the Acts 2 model is to help care for the needs of others.* During the early days of the Church, many disciples of Christ lost their families, jobs, and all means of support for themselves when they were baptized with water. This is still true in many cultures today. To be baptized in water meant that they renounced their old way of life, and many were totally disowned and rejected by their families. The need was very real and extreme for some. Therefore, those who had the means and the resources provided the shelter, food, clothing, etc., to those brothers and sisters with such a need in the Church.

We all need to have a group that we can depend on for help in time of need. This is especially true today with the potential increase in persecution and financial need that may erupt in the days ahead. We should be ready to help a needy or sick family with meals or other needs. This is what a family does!

When the Church begins to do what we were created to do, people under the influence of the world begin to take notice of how different we are. As a result, they are drawn by the love they see exhibited, as "they will know us by our love" (see John 15:35).

Fourth Aspect of Field #4: Team Ministry- Everyone Has A Job To Do

> *Having made known unto us the mystery of His will, according to His good pleasure which he has purposed in Himself: That in the dispensation of the fulness of times He might gather together in one all things in Christ, both which are in heaven, and which are on earth; even in Him:*
>
> — Ephesians 1:9-10

> *And has put all things under His feet, and gave Him to be the head over all things to the church, which is His body, the fulness of Him that fills all in all.*
>
> — Ephesians 1:22-23

> *And are built upon the foundation of the apostles and prophets, Jesus Christ Himself being the chief corner stone; In whom all the building fitly framed together grows unto an holy temple in the Lord: In whom you also are built together for a habitation of God through the Spirit.*
>
> — Ephesians 2:20-22

God has a master plan to bring everything in heaven and in

earth into unity based upon the Lordship and rule of Jesus Christ. This rule includes both the spirit and natural realms. Each of us have a unique role to play in this endeavor, as we are the only beings God created with both a spiritual aspect, our spirit, and a physical aspect, our body. As we co-labor with God, we have the ability to impact both the spirit and natural realms. We are to accomplish this stewardship as an individual and as a member of what the Bible calls a mystery, the EKKLESIA, which is the Church. We are uniquely made to be a bridge to bring to the physical earth the spiritual kingdom of God... on earth as it is in heaven.

> *For as we have many members in one body, and all members have not the same office: So we, being many, are one body in Christ, and every one members one of another. Having then gifts differing according to the grace that is given to us...*
>
> — ROMANS 12:4-6

In contrast to the Acts 2 Model, the most common Western Church model today consists of a pastor who leads the church with a few associate pastors and a handful of members who do all the work. The congregation is encouraged to attend Sunday meetings and to give an offering, but little else is expected of the congregation.

On the other hand, the biblical model we see in Ephesians 4:11-16 is quite different from the Western Church model in that every member of the church should be trained and prepared to do the work of the ministry. According to the Bible, this type of training is supposed to be done by those members who operate in five-fold ministry gifts who God has set in a church.

Each of us has something to bring to the local EKKLESIA. Every member brings different gifts, talents, and anointing which are to be used to serve everyone else. Everyone has a job to do and there is no room for benchwarmers. The Church was not created by God to be a passive group of spectators! His original intent was for His people to be energized by Holy Spirit to minister and to serve. Everyone is to contribute through team ministry and every member has a purpose and a job to do in this endeavor! We need each other in order to accomplish our individual purpose.

What is an example of the gifts God may have given you for use in the Church? Perhaps, God wants you to use the motivational gift which is placed in each of us. In Romans 12:5-8 we see that these gifts will manifest seven different ways as church members respond to help meet the needs of others. Perhaps God wants to use you through the manifestation gifts which are primarily used during Church services. However, these gifts may manifest at other places and times as well. In 1 Corinthians 12:7-14 we learn that everyone has the potential to be used by Holy Spirit in each of these gifts. God is merely looking for those who make themselves available and who will be obedient. Or perhaps you have a five-fold ministry calling which is used to help mature and equip the Church. This is given for lifelong use by ministers of the Gospel of the Kingdom. In Ephesians 4:11-16 we see these gifts are given to mature the Church, as well as to teach people how to minister to God, to fellow believers, to the unsaved, and to influence the world systems. These five-fold ministers also help to build up the Church, to bring unity, and to teach the knowledge of the Son of God. Their impact brings stability to keep everyone from being influenced by false doctrine, by devices of evil men, and by liars who are on assignment to destroy the Church.

> *But this is that which was spoken by the prophet Joel; And it shall come to pass in the last days, saith God, I will pour out of my Spirit upon all flesh: and your sons and your daughters shall prophesy, and your young men shall see visions, and your old men shall dream dreams: And on my servants and on my handmaidens I will pour out in those days of my Spirit; and they shall prophesy:*
>
> — ACT 2:16-18

> *And it shall come to pass,* that *whosoever shall call on the name of the Lord shall be saved.*
>
> — ACT 2:21

God prophetically established in Joel 2 and in Acts 2 His government for accomplishing the work of the New Testament Church. Everyone is to have an active role in the work of expanding the Kingdom of God. God sets an "old man", or a man who is wise in the things of the Kingdom as the set man, or pastor, for the local church. God gives this person the total dream, or vision of the big picture, for the direction and mission of the church. In due season, God raises up others to help accomplish it. The God-given dream is always too big for one person to accomplish, so God raises up young men and women who see visions and prophesy. These people "see" a portion of the dream which they are to help oversee and to work on in order to bring the dream into existence. Then, the rest of the Body, expressed as servants and handmaidens, help the young men and women do the work required to accomplish it. Please consider the following principles:

- There is only one dream, or overall vision for a church, which is given by God to the set man.
- Everyone needs to submit to the set man and help bring the vision into existence.
- Some young men and women, generally those who are 20-40 years old, will be given a vision of part of the dream which they are uniquely gifted and empowered to accomplish. This vision and prophesy must line up with the set man's dream or it will bring confusion.
- Everyone in the church is to help in the work of the vision. There are no fans or spectators in the Kingdom.
- God is always given the glory for the results!

MEMORY SCRIPTURE

1Corinthians 12:18, 27 *But now hath God set the members every one of them in the body, as it has pleased him. Now you are the Body of Christ, and members in particular.*

QUESTIONS TO PONDER

1. Did you know that God expects believers to gather together on a regular basis with a church?
2. Did you know that God expects you to live a

lifestyle separated from those who are not saved?
3. What are your spiritual gifts and how are they supposed to function in serving your local church?

WHAT GOD SAYS ABOUT YOU

Write your answer in a notebook.

1. Read 1 Corinthians 12:1; Hebrews 10:22-25- write down the different gifts which are used to serve the church.
2. Read Genesis 12:1; Isaiah 52:11; Jeremiah 51:6- write down what God says we are to do about living life as those who are unsaved live.
3. Read Acts 2:15-18; 1 Corinthians 12; Ephesians 2:19-22; Ephesians 4:1-8- write down the different gifts which you may have.

BECOMING WHO GOD CREATED YOU TO BE

1. Seriously begin to seek God in prayer for direction of where He would have you to be in church.
2. Meet with your pastor or mentor to discuss the vision for the church. Pray about what areas you are supposed to help to fulfill the vision.
3. After knowing where God has set you, commit to serve the church in every way the Lord shows you. Commit your tithes, offerings, resources, gifts, talents, and abilities. There is no such thing as a benchwarmer in the Kingdom of God.

CHAPTER TWELVE
THE FIELD OF OUR RELATIONSHIP WITH THE WORLD

> "Christians in this country have found themselves under selective assault. God has, almost overnight, been removed from the educational, legal, and political institutions of the country."
> -Rabbi Daniel Lapin, "America's Real War"[1]

God's original intent for His people has always been for us, who are made in His likeness and image, to be His representatives on the earth. We are given the mission to fill the whole earth with the knowledge and the glory of God. This includes making known who He is, what He is like, and how His Kingdom operates, as well as how He feels about different things and what motivates Him.

In Matthew 6:33 Jesus gave us insight into two aspects of how this mandate is to be focused as we, ..." seek you first the kingdom of God, and His righteousness." The context of this scripture deals specifically with the conflict between serving God, and His kingdom, in opposition to serving mammon and the world systems which are influenced by darkness. As a result, Christians are to be cultural activists who are destined to transform and influence all aspects of culture in order to reflect the nature of God. This is expressed in Mark 16:15-20 as Jesus spoke clearly of His intent for us to, ..."go you into all the world". The Greek word translated "world" is KOSMOS, which is always used biblically to describe arenas and world systems where Satan attempts to exert influence. We see from this word that our commission is to enact change in the culture God has placed us in.

> *For the earth shall be filled with the knowledge of the glory of the LORD, as the waters cover the sea.*
>
> — HABAKKUK 2:14

Historically, the Church has been the driving force for cultural reform. For example[2], the first hospitals, hospices, orphanages, and nursing homes were founded by Christians. Christianity is all about taking the Gospel of the Kingdom to the hurting, the poor, and those who are not able to help themselves. The great revivalist Charles Finney led many people to Jesus over the course of His ministry. His message included both the evangelistic message and the Christian responsibility for cultural reform. As a result, many of his disciples left their jobs and went to work in hospitals, orphanages, charities that fed the poor, etc. Cultural change was the fruit of his ministry and should be our fruit as well!

The second area[3] of our influence in Matthew 6:33 is to share His righteousness as we actively make disciples of those who are living in darkness, pain, and oppression. This is addressed in Matthew 28:19-20 which directs us to, ..."go and teach all nations". The word "teach" is the Greek word MATHETEUO which means to make a disciple (never a convert), and the word "nations" which is the Greek word ETHNOS which refers to all ethnic, racial, and culture groups. This assignment is to be done in direct opposition to the spiritual desolation and darkness that is the result of the fall of man in the Garden of Eden.

The Field of Relationship with the World

Our relationship with world systems deals with the government of our individual purpose in dealing with the desolation and darkness in a fallen world. We are given the responsibility for spreading the Kingdom of God and its influence throughout the earth. This determines how we are to deal with relationships in our sphere of influence in the marketplace, on our jobs, with our neighbors, or with relatives. We are also responsible for influencing the culture with the principles of the Kingdom.

How are we going to fulfill our purpose in this field? God gives each of us everything needed to accomplish this from the obedience and transformation which we walk through in each of the other four fields. We have the goods as a result of our faithfulness in those relationships. Therefore, we should be empowered to:

1. co-labor with Him as we rule and reign as an overcomer of sin and of darkness in the world.
2. physically go and to take the light into the darkest places of sin and wickedness.

3. pray prophetically as He speaks to us and become His intercessors for the nations.
4. stand in direct opposition to evil, wickedness, and oppression in our lives, in our culture, and in world systems.
5. preach and teach the Gospel of the Kingdom to all men in order to make disciples.

First Aspect of Field #5: Our Mission to Take Light Into Darkness

> *For, behold, the darkness shall cover the earth, and gross darkness the people: but the LORD shall arise upon thee, and his glory shall be seen upon thee.*
>
> — Isaiah 60:2

The Church's mission is to co-labor[4] with God in repairing the broken systems and lives of those under satanic influences. The Hebrew word TIKKAN is often used to describe this process, which means to repair, to fix, and to restore something. As a result, the overall impact of our efforts should be to make people's lives, the culture, and the world better than it ever was. TIKKAN describes what Jesus was sent to do through His ministry of reconciliation. He was sent to bring light into the darkness, and He in turn sends us to do the same thing!

However, we need to be aware[5] of the danger of the philosophies of men that are widely accepted as truth today. These hinder our mission! For example, one such philosophy, Escapism, is very prominent today. Escapism is based upon taking the belief in dispensationalism and the imminent return of Christ to the extreme. This line of reasoning includes a belief that we are in the last days; therefore, Jesus is coming back to rapture us out of the darkness at any moment. There is no need to influence the systems of the world. After all, what sense does it make to polish the brass fixtures on a sinking ship. Instead of focusing on making disciples, which takes time and hard work, we need to make as many converts as possible since we are running out of time.

One problem with Escapism is that the Bible teaches that only one being knows the exact time Jesus is coming back. That would be Father God, and He is not telling anyone. So, we have no idea if this is going to be anytime soon or not. Beware of making prophetic scriptures say what we want them to say. Another problem is that Jesus clearly told us that we are to make disciples, not converts. There is a major difference! Escapism neuters the true mission of the Church, which is to actively influence cultures with the Kingdom of God as well as to make disciples in all people groups.

Second Aspect of Field #5: We Are to do What Jesus Did

> *... verily, I say unto you, He that believes on Me, the works that I do shall he do also; and **greater** works than these shall he do; because I go unto My Father. And whatever you shall ask in My name, that will I do, that the Father may be glorified in the Son.*
>
> — John 14:12-13

> *How God anointed Jesus of Nazareth with the Holy Ghost and with power: Who went about doing good and healing all that were oppressed of the devil; for God was with Him.*
>
> — Act 10:38

God's heart is for His people to freely give everyone access to the knowledge of who He is, of His lovingkindness and mercy, and of His provision and goodness that He gives His people. This is done as we follow the example that Jesus set for us to follow. To do this effectively, we must first trust that what God says about us is true. For example, do we really believe what John 14 says in that we are to do the same works that Jesus did? This scripture actually says that we will do greater works? Yes, or no? This is critical to fulfilling our destiny, and we must learn to identify ourselves "in Christ" and go about doing what He is calling us to do.

In Acts 10, Jesus was anointed by God with the Holy Ghost and with power. This comes from only one place, by waiting upon the Lord! Maintaining a life where we consistently BARAK is just as essential today as it was at creation! There is no substitute. We all need the power of God to accomplish our purpose, for flesh and blood are never enough. Please be aware that there are many who are currently teaching about the Father, Son, and the Bible, totally ignoring the ministry of Holy Spirit, which leads to another gospel which produces a form of Godliness without the power of God. From all indications, and contrary to this mindset, Holy Spirit has not retired from being active in the lives of His people!

We all need to be taught the full gospel of the Bible, which includes understanding our relationship with each member of the Trinity of God (the Father, the Son, and the Holy Spirit). There has been a considerable amount of revelation taught about our relationship with the Father and the Son over the centuries; however the Church today has little understanding of Who Holy Spirit is and what He does. It is the author's opinion that God is rectifying this in our day, as He is giving His remnant fresh revelation of Holy Spirit's power and presence. For example, whenever we testify the Gospel of the Kingdom, the Holy Spirit co-labors with us by making His power available to testify as well. As a practical matter, in order to do the works that Jesus has told us to do, we need to understand how to recognize and co-labor with this power of Holy Spirit when we testify!

What are the works Jesus did? Everywhere He "went about doing good"! The Greek word[6] used for the phrase, "went about" gives us a picture of one's daily activities. This implies that Jesus did what He did as an overflow of His normal daily life. This also implies that He was aware that every encounter was orchestrated by Holy Spirit for the purpose of being ministered to. This should be our attitude as well, that everyone I encounter is brought to me to minister the Gospel of the Kingdom.

The first fruit born from the Holy Spirit's influence in Acts 10:38 is that Jesus daily went about doing good. The Greek word EUERGETEO is translated here as "good". This is an aspect of the fruit of the spirit which operated powerfully in Jesus' life. This word denotes someone who is a benefactor, a philanthropist, or one who financially supports charitable works. This word was used exclusively for someone who possessed great financial wealth and who helped support those in need.

It is clear from this that Jesus was a person of great wealth who used His resources to do good works. He cared for the poor, fed those in need, and helped to meet other basic needs of those who could not help themselves.

Jesus is our example for helping those who are in need, and He longs to do the same thing through us. The Church historically has been the source for aid to those in need. Christians founded the first hospitals, orphanages, hospices, adoption agencies, feeding programs, pro-life counseling services, etc. In the days ahead, the Church will be called upon to stand against tyranny and oppression at every level. Due to the implementation of oppressive government policies, there may be those who are denied access to a job to provide for their family, denied access to purchase food, and/or denied access to medical care. In such cases, God calls on His Church to stand up and help provide for those in need.

The second fruit born by the spirit in Jesus' daily life was that He healed all who were oppressed by the devil. As His Body, we are to make ourselves available at all times to be used to minister physical healings, to lead others to spiritual healing through our testimony and preaching the gospel, and to minister healing to the soul for those who need help. This will require us to become bold and to fear God more than we fear the rejection of man.

The lovingkindness of God ignites us to action in this part of our mission. This is birthed from spending time waiting on the Lord, and it is the fruit of the Holy Spirit which manifests in our life.

To fulfill our mission, we must make spending time with God our priority in life. His Spirit begins to change us and empowers us to give resources to those in need and to influence the cultures in the world for Christ. Holy Spirit also empowers

Third Aspect Field #5: How to deal with Government

<u>Four Types of Government</u>

It is important[7] for the believer to understand that there are biblically four types of government we deal with in life. The first type of government is the individual who exercises self-discipline. This is primarily[8] an issue of getting our body, soul, and spirit in proper order. Those who are born again can do this correctly and may experience an excellent quality of life based upon the self-discipline that flows from a spirit in communion with God. When a nation has a populace who walk in self-discipline, there will be little need for restrictions placed on personal liberty. The recognition of this truth is stated in the Declaration of Independence, as we all have the right from God to life, liberty and the pursuit of happiness. In addition, who and how we worship is a biblical right given to the individual.

The second type of government is the family. This is the authority given by God to the husband and wife who work together to raise their children. The parents have full responsibility for providing for, for protecting, and for teaching their children.

The third type of government is the Church. The Church has authority to gather together, to worship, and to teach the whole counsel of God contained within the Bible. This includes the authority to minister to God, to the saved, to the unsaved and to the cultural systems of order.

The fourth type of government is civil government. Civil

government is responsible for protecting good people from the actions of evil men, and to punish wicked and evil behavior. It is also responsible for protecting human life. The mutual self-defense of the nation and making provision for a peaceful society are also civil government's responsibility.

Anytime one of these four areas of government takes steps that encroach upon the God-given responsibility and authority of any of the other areas, it is out of order and must be corrected.

Responsibility of Christians to Civil Government

1. 1 Timothy 2:1-2- We all have the responsibility to pray for all those in authority over our nation, including our president. The focus and impact of our lives and the prayers of the Church should result in peace for the land. If the Church does its job, the fear of God will increase in the land and the people will live in peace. Great joy comes on the people when there is a leader who is righteous and rules accordingly. Proverbs 29:2 - Our actions should reflect our prayers as we become peacemakers in the land.
2. Titus 3:1- Believers should be model citizens, obeying the laws of the land and doing good works as much as is possible. However, this is limited to those laws which do not violate the morals and standards as established by God's Word.
3. Romans 13:6-7 - Believers are to pay taxes and the tribute they owe to help support the government.

4. I Peter 2:13- Believers are to show honor to all non-believers, to love our brothers in Christ, and to fear God.
5. Proverbs 29:2- Believers are to run for political office in nations that allow them to run. Due to the ungodliness and corruption of secular government, any believer running for office should be financially secure, have a strong marriage, and have a strong faith in the Lord.

Dealing With Foolish Kings

The fool hath said in his heart, There is *no God.* *They are corrupt, they have done abominable works,* there is *none that doeth good.*

— Psalm 14:1

There are times when a foolish king comes into power and encroaches upon the authority of the other areas of God-given government. The Bible defines a fool as a person who believes that God does not exist. In such cases where these kings blatantly violate the Word of God, such as the issue of making abortion legal, the Church is called to shine the light into the darkness and to stand up and be heard. Without being the salt for the culture, it will continue to decay even further. Jesus Himself refused to quit preaching when the Sandhedrin, the law-making body of Jerusalem, told Him to stop.

The first century Church did not passively accept[9] the evil practices of the Roman Empire. Instead, the Church stood in direct opposition by making a stand with marriage, a man and a woman getting married and having intimacy with only their spouse instead of the cultural norm of having multiple sex partners; by serving and worshipping only God and in refusing to participate in emperor and pagan worship; by resisting the infanticide of babies who were left to die under bridges by rescuing them in order to adopt and to raise as their own; and by confessing Jesus as King of Kings and refusing to proclaim Caesar as king of kings. These are just a few of the ways the Church influenced this evil empire. Eventually the empire changed to embrace much of what the Christians stood for.

Today, there are governments ruled by foolish kings in many nations that have passed laws and mandates that prohibit the Gospel of the Kingdom of God from being preached. This is the law of the land! On the other hand, the King of Kings has given us His Word, which is the law of the Kingdom, to preach the Gospel to the people of that nation. This is the law of the Kingdom of God! So, what do we do? There is a time, and a place, for Christian civil disobedience.

When foolish kings come to power, what is the proper biblical response for believers? In Romans 13:1-2, it is clear that we should do everything we can to be obedient to the laws of the land. But this does not mean we must violate the clear mandates of the Word of God. This is nonnegotiable! We are not to put any other gods before God! However, Romans 13 says the government's laws and mandates should be followed.

Please keep in mind[10] that tyrants, including Adolf Hitler and Karl Marx, have historically made Romans 13:1 one of the most abused scriptures in the Bible. They have successfully taken this scripture out of context to brow beat people into submitting to them. The foolish king's argument has been that whether the government is good, bad, evil, or indifferent, Christians are required by the Bible to shut up and submit to all government acts. Many people complied to their detriment! The tragedy is that most people didn't realize that this scripture describes a type of voluntary submission, not forced submission to civil authority. Romans 13:1 actually defines this type of submission as being conditional upon the government doing the right thing biblically. The sad thing is that the Church vacated its' rightful place of standing in opposition to evil through the misinterpretation of one scripture. Literally, millions lost their lives as a result.

The word translated "subject" in Romans 13:1 is the Greek word HUPOTASSO, the same word[11] used for a wife who voluntarily submits to the leadership of her husband in the Lord. This word means to come into proper military rank and file, to come into order. This is voluntary submission and is conditional. For example, this usage in the marriage relationship does not require the wife to submit to being abused by her husband, or of participating with him in sin at his insistence. She does not have to put up with this! Neither does a believer have to passively put up with evil in government.

So, what do we do when the foolish kings stand in direct opposition to God? Please consider this true story of one way to deal with this.

"Welcome to Mexico"! Everyone on the mission team read the sign with joy as they crossed the border into Mexico. The leader of the team had previously spent ten years on the mission field in Mexico, Nicaragua, and Guatemala, and had never lost the fire to preach the Gospel of the Kingdom to Hispanic and to Indian culture groups. As a result of his passion, he annually led groups to go south of the border to minister.

Those mission trips usually focused upon a prayer assignment as well as ministering the Word in churches, schools, home groups, on the streets, or in private homes. Missionaries in the local area worked with the team. The Lord moved mightily on those trips, and many team members were changed forever by what they saw and experienced. Much fruit of the Kingdom was also brought forth through the salvations, healings, and baptisms of the Holy Spirit that the nationals experienced. The work of the missionaries was strengthened as well!

What made these mission trips remarkable? Often, these were in direct violation of the laws of the land. In some areas missionaries were not even allowed in the country, and those who went anyway had to declare themselves as a tourist in order to enter the country. Needless to say, everyone was seriously compelled to hear the voice of God about being a member of the team.

There were many situations that occurred where the grace and protection of God manifested. On one trip in particular while in a small town in Mexico, one of the villagers invited the team to come to their house to lead a Bible study. Upon their arrival, the team sat down on the front porch. The temperature was well over 100 degrees, and it would have been very uncomfortable indoors. Please understand, that holding the Bible study was in direct disobedience to the rule of law, and the team's safety was at stake as they were visible for anyone to see.

The Bible study had been going well for some time, when a man could be seen in the distance walking toward the house. He was armed with a rifle, which was unusual in that area. He was walking directly toward the house! The leader ignored the man and continued teaching while the rest of the team prayed quietly in the spirit. Please understand, everyone knew God had spoken for them to be at that place, at that time, and with those people.

Meanwhile, the man continued to walk directly toward the

porch. As he grew closer, he began to angle to his left which led him to walk between where the Bible study was and the house next door. He never looked up or acknowledged that he saw what was going on. It was as though he never saw the group who was having the Bible study.

The members of the team had waited upon the Lord, heard His directions, obeyed explicitly what he said for them to do, had been witnesses of the Kingdom of God, and had worked to make disciples of men. Rest assured that when God speaks and gives direction to His people, He knows how to protect them! Not one hair on our heads can be touched unless it is His will.

God has called us to co-labor with Him in repairing the broken systems of the world, which often requires us to take a stand against insane kings. God's plan is not accomplished by taking dominion over a nation through armed revolution, but rather through making one disciple at a time. We are also called to influence the institutions that make up the culture of the nation with the Kingdom of God. If we are faithful to listen and to obey, we will be the light that shines into the darkness. This is our destiny! We are to be a blessing to the nations!

Conclusion to Yield to Yield

The parable of the mustard seed in Matthew 13:31-32, is the epitome of what Yield to Yield is all about. In order for us to enter into the Kingdom of God we must first accept in faith the seed, or the Word, which we hear through the foolishness of preaching. If we are being drawn by the convicting power of Holy Spirit, we may choose to receive this seed into our heart. This is done by fully surrendering our life to Jesus, as we make Him Lord and Savior of everything in our life. Through His redemptive sacrifice made on the cross, we receive forgiveness for all of our sins and are restored to God's fellowship and original purpose for our life. We are born again, and He makes all things new. But this is not an end in itself, but rather is the beginning of the process of sanctification through which our souls are transformed into His image.

The process of sanctification is a lifelong endeavor of working out our salvation with fear and trembling. This is done through the discipline of seeking God's presence and His voice, and through worshiping Him. This includes renewing our minds by studying and memorizing the Bible, as well as in gathering with fellow believers in order to fellowship and to eat together. Discipline progressively leads to a change in our lives as we become more like Him. That is, we yield ourselves fully in surrendering everything to Him. This allows Him to do His will in our life!

God's purpose is for us to first take the seeds of the Kingdom of God and to cultivate them in our own lives. Only then can we cultivate them in our families, our churches, and ultimately in the world. If we faithfully follow His daily instructions we will yield, or produce, a great physical and spiritual harvest as the seeds we plant germinate and bear fruit. The three seeds we are to manage are the seeds of rule, of the body, and of production.

According to the Bible, all of creation is waiting for the manifestation of the sons of God to re-emerge to bring everything back into order (Romans 8:18-22). Whether it happens in our generation or not, there will be a generation who will faithfully accomplish this. The Bible teaches that God is currently looking across the earth for those who He can show himself strong in (2 Chronicles 16:9). If this is true, why not our generation? Why not now?

God is currently raising up a remnant army of those who are willing to stand and to be counted as His sons. These people will commit to come out and separate themselves from the world and will be fully persuaded that they are hand-picked by Him for a special purpose. We are a people destined to an eternal future, who have great value in the eyes of God, and who have been empowered by the resurrection power of the Holy Spirit. We are directed to get our identification in Christ alone, and not from the things or relationships of the world (Ephesians 1-2).

Today, God is raising up His army to cultivate the harvest of people who He is breathing His breath upon. All He requires from us is to pray and ask for His burden for the lost, and then to go in obedience and in power as we make disciples of men. This mission includes influencing every system of order in the nations of the world. We are to accomplish this by being in unity with Him and with the members of the Body of Christ. By spending time with Him daily in fellowship, we will be filled with the lovingkindness of God. This is God's provision of a spiritual weapon against all wicked systems of the world, who have nothing that can stand against the love of God that overflows from us!

It is time for us to properly prepare ourselves for war by:

1. being serious about renewing our mind. It is not enough to know what the Word says. He expects us to read, meditate, and study the Word of God to the point that we make it our own and begin to think like He thinks.
2. seriously reconsider how we manage our finances, and make sure this lines up with His definition of us as being a giver and not a taker.

3. disciplining our tongue to speak forth life and the message of the kingdom, instead of the selfishness of the flesh or the fear mongering of the satanically influenced world systems.
4. becoming a worshipper of God.
5. accepting our responsibility for the education of our children. It is a God-given responsibility for parents, not the government, to educate or to oversee the education of children.
6. accepting God's perspective that all people including our spouse, members of the church, and those in the world are very valuable and are worth serving.
7. cutting lifelong covenant relationships with God, our spouse. and with our church.
8. seriously accepting admonition to go to work serving in the church God sets us in.
9. being willing to eat with and to fellowship with believers.
10. becoming a spiritual force to be reckoned with in going out to make disciples and to engage in cultural reform. We are called to fix what is broken!

In Genesis 10:8-10, Nimrod was the first foolish king[12] mentioned in the Bible. Jewish historians teach that he was a mighty hunter of animals as well as men, and that his heart was totally set upon evil and wickedness. He aggressively sought out believers to influence to follow him instead of God. As a result, many turned their back on serving God.

In Genesis 12:1-3, the Abrahamic blessing was God's antidote to the evil of Nimrod. It is the author's opinion that this blessing is God's provision of a spiritual weapon of mass destruction for use against all wicked systems of the world. Furthermore, Jesus has made this blessing available to us today (Galatians 3:5-9,14. However, we need to understand this is conditional since He requires us to separate ourselves from the world system. It is up to each of us!

We need to understand that God blesses those who separate from the world! What is the result? He promises to make us a nation, which increases our influence, resources, and the impact of our lives on others. He blesses us with spiritual and physical prosperity and makes our name great before men. This results in respect and honor in our lives as we bare the image and likeness of God.

The Abrahamic blessing equips us to influence the nations. How? God makes us a blessing to others! Those who bless us will in turn be blessed, and those who curse us will be cursed. But more importantly, God gives us the vision that we are a blessing to all the families on the earth.

The Abrahamic blessing is the foundation of the concept of Yield to Yield. God does a work in each of us, which in turn allows us to do the work of the Kingdom on earth. This is our destiny!

MEMORY VERSE

Habakkuk 2:14 *For the earth shall be filled with the knowledge of the glory of the LORD, as the waters cover the sea.*

QUESTIONS TO PONDER

1. Do you realize that it is biblically and historically

the Church's responsibility to stand in opposition to evil and wicked men?
2. Did you know that God has commissioned His Church to fix, repair, and make better than new the broken cultures in the world?
3. Do you understand that God is looking for those who will co-labor with Him in being a world changer?

WHAT GOD SAYS ABOUT YOU

Write answers in a notebook.

1. Read Matthew 6:33; Mark 16:15-20; Matthew 28:19-10 and reread the first three pages of this chapter. Write down the directions He gives for us to follow in outreach.
2. Read Acts 10:38; John 14:12;- write down what Jesus did as He ministered to the lost. What are we supposed to do according to these scriptures?
3. Read Genesis 10:8-11, 12:1-3; Galatians 3:5-9, 14- write down the seven aspects of the blessing of Abraham. Who has access to these blessings today?

BECOMING WHO GOD CREATED YOU TO BE

1. Discuss with your pastor or mentor how to witness the Gospel of the Kingdom to the lost. Begin to minister to everyone in your sphere of influence.

2. As a part of your daily discipline- ask Holy Spirit to show you who you need to minister to today.
3. Become prepared to invest time, money, and energy in making disciples. There are those who are desperately searching for what you have, but won't currently go to a church. Commit to meet with them, listen to them, let them cry on your shoulder, become their friend, etc. What speaks to people is not what we say, but rather how much we really care about them. Remember, ministry comes out of relationship.

Acknowledgments

"The Lord gave the word: great was the company of those that published it."

— Psalm 68:11 KJV

The Bible teaches that we are all one Body and that different members bring different gifts and talents that benefit the other members. This is especially true of the team of individuals who have influenced or had a direct hand in creating this book. I want to say thank you and "God bless you", to all those who have helped make publishing this book a reality.

First, I want to say thank you to the woman of my dreams, Harriet my wife of 44 years. Without your encouragement and willingness to sacrifice a significant amount of time with your husband, this book would never have gotten off the ground. Also, your sweet grammar police skills have been greatly appreciated.

Thank you to my pastor, Dr. Mack Ballard, who has consistently prayed for and encouraged me to get this project completed. Also, I want to thank my other mentors who have sown the seeds of truth into my life over the years. This is true of, but not limited to, Dr. Benny Charles Hand, Dr. Ron Cottle, Dr. Ed Nelson, and Pastor Steve Vickers. If nothing else, this book should encourage each of you that at least one of your students was listening whenever you preached or taught.

Also, I would like to give special thanks to Adam Davis for your anointed guidance, expertise, and input that I personally needed to complete Yield to Yield.

Thank you to each member of Fountain Gate Church of Auburn, Alabama for being a blessing in my life. This is especially true of those overcomers who have taken what I have taught which is in this book and applied it in your lives.

I especially want to glorify and thank God for being my Lord and Savior, and for allowing me to serve Him in writing His book, Yield to Yield. All the glory goes to Him!

About the Author

Dr. Dan Lane has served God as a pastor since 1986, and he is currently the Senior Pastor of Fountain Gate Church in Auburn, Alabama. He also gives direction and counsel to pastors in the southeast. He brings with him years of experience as a self-employed businessman; as principal emeritus of Ballard Christian School; 20 years as hospital chaplain; as President of Monteagle Institute of Theology; and as the host of the radio program Choose Life.

He holds a bachelor's degree from Auburn University, a Doctor of Ministry degree from Christian Life School of Theology, and a Doctor of Theology degree from Monteagle Institute of Theology.

Following the direction of the Lord, he sold his business in 1986 in order to answer the call to ministry and has been in full-time ministry ever since. Dan has been married to his childhood sweetheart Harriet since 1978, and she has faithfully supported him in ministry over the years. They have three children of their own who they homeschooled, as well as several grandchildren. They also have many other spiritual children they have raised together.

Dan's burning passion is to teach and to equip the generations to fulfill their God-given purpose for being born, and in the process to call the Church to embrace and activate its destiny!

For more information or to contact Dr. Lane, visit www.YieldtoYieldBook.com.

NOTES

1. Chapter One

1. Robert J. Morgan, *Preacher's Sourcebook for Creative Sermon Illustrations* (Nashville, TN: Thomas Nelson, 2007), 818.
2. Robert J. Morgan, *Preacher's Sourcebook for Creative Sermon Illustrations* (Nashville, TN: Thomas Nelson, 2007), 820.
3. Spiros Zodhiates and Warren Baker, *Hebrew-Greek Key Word Study Bible: Key Insights into God's Word: King James Version, Authorized Version* (Chattanooga, TN: AMG Publishers, 2008).
4. Rick Renner, *Sparkling Gems from the Greek: 365 Greek Word Studies for Every Day of the Year to Sharpen Your Understanding of God's Word* (Tulsa, OK: Teach All Nations, 2003), 403.
5. Richard Stearns, *Hole in Our Gospel - What Does God Expect of Us? the Answer That Changed My* (Thomas Nelson Publishers, 2010), 17.
6. Brian Sanders, *Underground Church: A Living Example of the Church in Its Most Potent Form* (Grand Rapids, MI: Zondervan, 2018), 33.
7. Jeff A. Benner, *The Ancient Hebrew Lexicon of the Bible: Hebrew Letters, Words and Roots Defined within Their Ancient Cultural Context* (College Station, TX: Virtualbookworm.com Publishing, 2005).
8. Jeff A. Benner, *The Ancient Hebrew Lexicon of the Bible: Hebrew Letters, Words and Roots Defined within Their Ancient Cultural Context* (College Station, TX: Virtualbookworm.com Publishing, 2005).

2. Chapter Two

1. Cory, Lloyd. Essay. In *Quotable Quotations*, 316. Wheaton, IL: Victor Books, 1985.
2. Brown, Francis, S. R. Driver, Charles A. Briggs, Edward Robinson, Wilhelm Gesenius, and Maurice A. Robinson. Essay. In *The New Brown-Driver-Briggs-Gesenius Hebrew and English Lexicon: With an Appendix Containing Biblical Aramaic*, 921-922. Peabody, MA: Hendrickson, 1979.
3. Brown, Francis, S. R. Driver, Charles A. Briggs, Edward Robinson, Wilhelm Gesenius, and Maurice A. Robinson. Essay. In *The New Brown-Driver-Briggs-Gesenius Hebrew and English Lexicon: With an Appendix Containing Biblical Aramaic*, 915-916. Peabody, MA: Hendrickson, 1979.

4. Brown, Francis, S. R. Driver, Charles A. Briggs, Edward Robinson, Wilhelm Gesenius, and Maurice A. Robinson. Essay. In *The New Brown-Driver-Briggs-Gesenius Hebrew and English Lexicon: With an Appendix Containing Biblical Aramaic*, 712. Peabody, MA: Hendrickson, 1979.
5. Brown, Francis, S. R. Driver, Charles A. Briggs, Edward Robinson, Wilhelm Gesenius, and Maurice A. Robinson. Essay. In *The New Brown-Driver-Briggs-Gesenius Hebrew and English Lexicon: With an Appendix Containing Biblical Aramaic*, 1036. Peabody, MA: Hendrickson, 1979.
6. Brown, Francis, S. R. Driver, Charles A. Briggs, Edward Robinson, Wilhelm Gesenius, and Maurice A. Robinson. Essay. In *The New Brown-Driver-Briggs-Gesenius Hebrew and English Lexicon: With an Appendix Containing Biblical Aramaic*, 1036. Peabody, MA: Hendrickson, 1979.
7. Brown, Francis, S. R. Driver, Charles A. Briggs, Edward Robinson, Wilhelm Gesenius, and Maurice A. Robinson. Essay. In *The New Brown-Driver-Briggs-Gesenius Hebrew and English Lexicon: With an Appendix Containing Biblical Aramaic*, 1036. Peabody, MA: Hendrickson, 1979.
8. Brown, Francis, S. R. Driver, Charles A. Briggs, Edward Robinson, Wilhelm Gesenius, and Maurice A. Robinson. Essay. In *The New Brown-Driver-Briggs-Gesenius Hebrew and English Lexicon: With an Appendix Containing Biblical Aramaic*, 1036. Peabody, MA: Hendrickson, 1979.
9. Berlin, Adele, Marc Zvi Brettler, and Michael Fishbane. *The Jewish Study Bible: Jewish Publication Society Tanakh Translation*. Oxford: Oxford University Press, 2004.
10. Brown, Francis, S. R. Driver, Charles A. Briggs, Edward Robinson, Wilhelm Gesenius, and Maurice A. Robinson. Essay. In *The New Brown-Driver-Briggs-Gesenius Hebrew and English Lexicon: With an Appendix Containing Biblical Aramaic*, 638. Peabody, MA: Hendrickson, 1979.
11. "Jewishencyclopedia.com." FALL OF MAN - JewishEncyclopedia.com. Accessed February 14, 2022. https://jewishencyclopedia.com/articles/5999-fall-of-man.

3. Chapter Three

1. Cory, Lloyd. Essay. In *Quotable Quotations*, 322. Wheaton, IL: Victor Books, 1985.
2. esword Keil and Delitzsch Commentary of the Old Testament
3. Lapin, Rabbi Daniel. Essay. In *Thou Shall Prosper: Ten Commandments for Making Money, 2nd Edition*, 68-69. John Wiley & Sons, 2009.
4. Schmidt, Alvin J. Essay. In *How Christianity Changed the World*, 79-85. Grand Rapids, MI: Zondervan, 2004.
5. "Noah, Ham and the Curse of Canaan: Who Did What to Whom in the Tent?" TheTorah.com. Accessed February 14, 2022. https://www.

thetorah.com/article/noah-ham-and-the-curse-of-canaan-who-did-what-to-whom-in-the-tent.
6. "Jewishencyclopedia.com." NIMROD - JewishEncyclopedia.com. Accessed February 14, 2022. https://jewishencyclopedia.com/articles/11548-nimrod.
7. Commentary made by Dr. Ed Nelson taken from lecture notes
8. Zodhiates, Spiros, and Warren Baker. Essay. In *Hebrew-Greek Key Word Study Bible: Key Insights into God's Word: King James Version, Authorized Version*, 2164. Chattanooga, TN: AMG Publishers, 2008.

4. Chapter Four

1. Renner, Rick. Essay. In *Sparkling Gems from the Greek: 365 Greek Word Studies for Every Day of the Year to Sharpen Your Understanding of God's Word*, 39. Tulsa, OK: Teach All Nations, 2003.
2. Benner, Jeff A. *The Ancient Hebrew Lexicon of the Bible: Hebrew Letters, Words and Roots Defined within Their Ancient Cultural Context*. College Station, TX: Virtualbookworm.com Publishing, 2005.
3. Benner, Jeff A. *The Ancient Hebrew Lexicon of the Bible: Hebrew Letters, Words and Roots Defined within Their Ancient Cultural Context*. College Station, TX: Virtualbookworm.com Publishing, 2005.
4. Benner, Jeff A. *The Ancient Hebrew Lexicon of the Bible: Hebrew Letters, Words and Roots Defined within Their Ancient Cultural Context*. College Station, TX: Virtualbookworm.com Publishing, 2005.
5. Benner, Jeff A. *The Ancient Hebrew Lexicon of the Bible: Hebrew Letters, Words and Roots Defined within Their Ancient Cultural Context*. College Station, TX: Virtualbookworm.com Publishing, 2005.
6. Brown, Francis, S. R. Driver, Charles A. Briggs, Edward Robinson, Wilhelm Gesenius, and Maurice A. Robinson. Essay. In *The New Brown-Driver-Briggs-Gesenius Hebrew and English Lexicon: With an Appendix Containing Biblical Aramaic*, 803. Peabody, MA: Hendrickson, 1979.
7. Benner, Jeff A. *The Ancient Hebrew Lexicon of the Bible: Hebrew Letters, Words and Roots Defined within Their Ancient Cultural Context*. College Station, TX: Virtualbookworm.com Publishing, 2005.
8. Renner, Rick. Essay. In *Sparkling Gems from the Greek: 365 Greek Word Studies for Every Day of the Year to Sharpen Your Understanding of God's Word*, 737. Tulsa, OK: Teach All Nations, 2003.
9. Renner, Rick. Essay. In *Sparkling Gems from the Greek: 365 Greek Word Studies for Every Day of the Year to Sharpen Your Understanding of God's Word*, 276. Tulsa, OK: Teach All Nations, 2003.
10. Benner, Jeff A. *The Ancient Hebrew Lexicon of the Bible: Hebrew Letters, Words and Roots Defined within Their Ancient Cultural Context*. College Station, TX: Virtualbookworm.com Publishing, 2005.

11. Brown, Francis, S. R. Driver, Charles A. Briggs, Edward Robinson, Wilhelm Gesenius, and Maurice A. Robinson. Essay. In *The New Brown-Driver-Briggs-Gesenius Hebrew and English Lexicon: With an Appendix Containing Biblical Aramaic*, 876. Peabody, MA: Hendrickson, 1979.

5. Chapter Five

1. Thayer, Joseph Henry, Christian Gottlob Wilke, and Joseph Henry Thayer. *Greek-English Lexicon of the New Testament: Being Grimm's Wilke's Clavis Novi Testamenti*. Massachusetts: Hendrickson Pub., 1999.
2. Zodhiates, Spiros, and Warren Baker. Essay. In *Hebrew-Greek Key Word Study Bible: Key Insights into God's Word: King James Version, Authorized Version*, 2384. Chattanooga, TN: AMG Publishers, 2008.
3. Brown, Francis, S. R. Driver, Charles A. Briggs, Edward Robinson, Wilhelm Gesenius, and Maurice A. Robinson. Essay. In *The New Brown-Driver-Briggs-Gesenius Hebrew and English Lexicon: With an Appendix Containing Biblical Aramaic*. Peabody, MA: Hendrickson, 1979.
4. Smith, William, F. N. Peloubet, and Peloubet M A T. Essay. In *Smith's Bible Dictionary*, 532. Nashville, TN: T. Nelson, 1986.
5. Gill, John. *John Gill's Exposition of the Entire Bible*, 2012.
6. Gill, John. *John Gill's Exposition of the Entire Bible*, 2012.
7. Gill, John. *John Gill's Exposition of the Entire Bible*, 2012.
8. Gill, John. *John Gill's Exposition of the Entire Bible*, 2012.
9. Nee, Watchman. *The Normal Christian Worker*. Wheaton: Tyndale House, 1977.
10. Boice, James Montgomery. Essay. In *Foundations of the Christian Faith: A Comprehensive & Readable Theology*, 389. Downers Grove, IL: InterVarsity Press, 1986.
11. Boice, James Montgomery. Essay. In *Foundations of the Christian Faith: A Comprehensive & Readable Theology*, 390. Downers Grove, IL: InterVarsity Press, 1986.

6. Chapter Six

1. Lapin, Rabbi Daniel. Essay. In *Thou Shall Prosper: Ten Commandments for Making Money, 2nd Edition*, 337. John Wiley & Sons, 2009.
2. Renner, Rick. Essay. In *Sparkling Gems from the Greek: 365 Greek Word Studies for Every Day of the Year to Sharpen Your Understanding of God's Word*, 555-557. Tulsa, OK: Teach All Nations, 2003.
3. Benner, Jeff A. *The Ancient Hebrew Lexicon of the Bible: Hebrew Letters, Words and Roots Defined within Their Ancient Cultural Context*. College Station, TX: Virtualbookworm.com Publishing, 2005.

4. Brown, Francis, S. R. Driver, Charles A. Briggs, Edward Robinson, Wilhelm Gesenius, and Maurice A. Robinson. Essay. In *The New Brown-Driver-Briggs-Gesenius Hebrew and English Lexicon: With an Appendix Containing Biblical Aramaic*, 962. Peabody, MA: Hendrickson, 1979.
5. Zodhiates, Spiros, and Warren Baker. Essay. In *Hebrew-Greek Key Word Study Bible: Key Insights into God's Word: King James Version, Authorized Version*, 1865. Chattanooga, TN: AMG Publishers, 2008.
6. Brown, Francis, S. R. Driver, Charles A. Briggs, Edward Robinson, Wilhelm Gesenius, and Maurice A. Robinson. Essay. In *The New Brown-Driver-Briggs-Gesenius Hebrew and English Lexicon: With an Appendix Containing Biblical Aramaic*, 1036. Peabody, MA: Hendrickson, 1979.
7. Idleman, Kyle. Essay. In *Not a Fan: Becoming a Completely Committed Follower of Jesus*, 55. Grand Rapids, MI: Zondervan, 2011.
8. Benner, Jeff A. *The Ancient Hebrew Lexicon of the Bible: Hebrew Letters, Words and Roots Defined within Their Ancient Cultural Context*. College Station, TX: Virtualbookworm.com Publishing, 2005.
9. Smith, William, F. N. Peloubet, and Peloubet M A T. Essay. In *Smith's Bible Dictionary*, 425-426. Nashville, TN: T. Nelson, 1986.

7. Chapter Seven

1. Benner, Jeff A. *The Ancient Hebrew Lexicon of the Bible: Hebrew Letters, Words and Roots Defined within Their Ancient Cultural Context*. College Station, TX: Virtualbookworm.com Publishing, 2005.
2. Brown, Francis, S. R. Driver, Charles A. Briggs, Edward Robinson, Wilhelm Gesenius, and Maurice A. Robinson. Essay. In *The New Brown-Driver-Briggs-Gesenius Hebrew and English Lexicon: With an Appendix Containing Biblical Aramaic*, 26. Peabody, MA: Hendrickson, 1979.
3. Brown, Francis, S. R. Driver, Charles A. Briggs, Edward Robinson, Wilhelm Gesenius, and Maurice A. Robinson. Essay. In *The New Brown-Driver-Briggs-Gesenius Hebrew and English Lexicon: With an Appendix Containing Biblical Aramaic*, 442. Peabody, MA: Hendrickson, 1979.
4. Benner, Jeff A. *The Ancient Hebrew Lexicon of the Bible: Hebrew Letters, Words and Roots Defined within Their Ancient Cultural Context*. College Station, TX: Virtualbookworm.com Publishing, 2005.
5. Benner, Jeff A. *The Ancient Hebrew Lexicon of the Bible: Hebrew Letters, Words and Roots Defined within Their Ancient Cultural Context*. College Station, TX: Virtualbookworm.com Publishing, 2005.
6. *See* Ephesians 5:15, 21
7. Benner, Jeff A. *The Ancient Hebrew Lexicon of the Bible: Hebrew Letters, Words and Roots Defined within Their Ancient Cultural Context*. College Station, TX: Virtualbookworm.com Publishing, 2005.

8. Benner, Jeff A. *The Ancient Hebrew Lexicon of the Bible: Hebrew Letters, Words and Roots Defined within Their Ancient Cultural Context.* College Station, TX: Virtualbookworm.com Publishing, 2005.
9. Brown, Francis, S. R. Driver, Charles A. Briggs, Edward Robinson, Wilhelm Gesenius, and Maurice A. Robinson. Essay. In *The New Brown-Driver-Briggs-Gesenius Hebrew and English Lexicon: With an Appendix Containing Biblical Aramaic*, 804-805. Peabody, MA: Hendrickson, 1979.
10. Macmillan, D.D., H. "The Dew of Hermon." Biblehub.com. Accessed February 14, 2022. https://biblehub.com/sermons/auth/macmillan/the_dew_of_hermon.htm.

8. Chapter Eight

1. Hudson Taylor. AZQuotes.com, Wind and Fly LTD, 2022. https://www.azquotes.com/quote/544783, accessed February 14, 2022.
2. Stearns, Richard. Essay. In *The Hole in Our Gospel: What Does God Expect of Us?*, 104. Nashville, TN: Thomas Nelson, 2010.
3. Benner, Jeff A. *The Ancient Hebrew Lexicon of the Bible: Hebrew Letters, Words and Roots Defined within Their Ancient Cultural Context.* College Station, TX: Virtualbookworm.com Publishing, 2005.
4. Benner, Jeff A. *The Ancient Hebrew Lexicon of the Bible: Hebrew Letters, Words and Roots Defined within Their Ancient Cultural Context.* College Station, TX: Virtualbookworm.com Publishing, 2005.
5. Thayer, Joseph Henry, Christian Gottlob Wilke, and Joseph Henry Thayer. *Greek-English Lexicon of the New Testament: Being Grimm's Wilke's Clavis Novi Testamenti*. Massachusetts: Hendrickson Pub., 1999.
6. Dr. Ed Nelson lecture notes.
7. Berlin, Adele, Marc Zvi Brettler, and Michael Fishbane. *The Jewish Study Bible: Jewish Publication Society Tanakh Translation*. Oxford: Oxford University Press, 2004., page 15
8. *See* I Timothy 4:24
9. *See* Romans 10:9-10
10. *See* Acts 1:8
11. *See* Hebrews 10:19-22
12. Thayer, Joseph Henry, Christian Gottlob Wilke, and Joseph Henry Thayer. *Greek-English Lexicon of the New Testament: Being Grimm's Wilke's Clavis Novi Testamenti*. Massachusetts: Hendrickson Pub., 1999.
13. Brown, Francis, S. R. Driver, Charles A. Briggs, Edward Robinson, Wilhelm Gesenius, and Maurice A. Robinson. Essay. In *The New Brown-Driver-Briggs-Gesenius Hebrew and English Lexicon: With an Appendix Containing Biblical Aramaic*, 659. Peabody, MA: Hendrickson, 1979.
14. *See* 2 Corinthians 10:5

9. Chapter Nine

1. Lapin, Rabbi Daniel. Essay. In *Thou Shall Prosper: Ten Commandments for Making Money, 2nd Edition*, 300. John Wiley & Sons, 2009.
2. Lapin, Rabbi Daniel. Essay. In *Thou Shall Prosper: Ten Commandments for Making Money, 2nd Edition*, 50. John Wiley & Sons, 2009.
3. Ball, F. Nolan. Essay. In *God's Plan for Financing the Ministry*, 56. Panama City, FL: Rock of Panama City, Inc., 1992.
4. Lapin, Rabbi Daniel. Essay. In *Thou Shall Prosper: Ten Commandments for Making Money, 2nd Edition*, 316. John Wiley & Sons, 2009.
5. Batterson, Mark. Essay. In *Double Blessing: How to Get It, How to Give It*, 134. Colorado Springs, CO: Multnomah, an imprint of Random House, 2019.
6. See Acts 16:19, I Kings 19:12, I Timothy 4:14, Luke 1:28, Matthew 3:17,
7. Dr. Benny Charles Hand lecture notes

10. Chapter Ten

1. Smith, William, F. N. Peloubet, and Peloubet M A T. Essay. In *Smith's Bible Dictionary*, 382–84. Nashville, TN: T. Nelson, 1986.
2. ibid page 156
3. from Dr. Ed Nelson lecture notes
4. Morgan, Robert J. Essay. In *Preacher's Sourcebook for Creative Sermon Illustrations*, 530. Nashville, TN: Thomas Nelson, 2007.
5. Schmidt, Alvin J. Essay. In *How Christianity Changed the World*, 100-102. Grand Rapids, MI: Zondervan, 2004.
6. Berlin, Adele, Marc Zvi Brettler, and Michael Fishbane. *The Jewish Study Bible: Jewish Publication Society Tanakh Translation*. Oxford: Oxford University Press, 2004, page 16
7. Schmidt, Alvin J. Essay. In *How Christianity Changed the World*, 83. Grand Rapids, MI: Zondervan, 2004.
8. ibid, page 27
9. Mansfield, Stephen. Essay. In *Mansfield's Book of Manly Men*, 221. Nashville, TN: Thomas Nelson, 2013.
10. Thayer, Joseph Henry, Christian Gottlob Wilke, and Joseph Henry Thayer. *Greek-English Lexicon of the New Testament: Being Grimm's Wilke's Clavis Novi Testamenti*. Massachusetts: Hendrickson Pub., 1999.
11. Benner, Jeff A. *The Ancient Hebrew Lexicon of the Bible: Hebrew Letters, Words and Roots Defined within Their Ancient Cultural Context*. College Station, TX: Virtualbookworm.com Publishing, 2005.

11. Chapter Eleven

1. Idleman, Kyle. Essay. In *Not a Fan: Becoming a Completely Committed Follower of Jesus*, 55. Grand Rapids, MI: Zondervan, 2011.
2. lecture notes Dr. Benny Charles Hand
3. Brown, Francis, S. R. Driver, Charles A. Briggs, Edward Robinson, Wilhelm Gesenius, and Maurice A. Robinson. Essay. In *The New Brown-Driver-Briggs-Gesenius Hebrew and English Lexicon: With an Appendix Containing Biblical Aramaic*, 136. Peabody, MA: Hendrickson, 1979.
4. Joseph Henry Thayer, Christian Gottlob Wilke, and Joseph Henry Thayer, *Greek-English Lexicon of the New Testament: Being Grimm's Wilke's Clavis Novi Testamenti* (Massachusetts: Hendrickson Pub., 1999).
5. Kevin J. Conner, in *The Church in the New Testament* (Chichester, Eng.: Sovereign World, 1989), page 24
6. Joseph Henry Thayer, Christian Gottlob Wilke, and Joseph Henry Thayer, *Greek-English Lexicon of the New Testament: Being Grimm's Wilke's Clavis Novi Testamenti* (Massachusetts: Hendrickson Pub., 1999).
7. Kevin J. Conner, in *The Church in the New Testament* (Chichester, Eng.: Sovereign World, 1989), page 21
8. Kevin J. Conner, in *The Church in the New Testament* (Chichester, Eng.: Sovereign World, 1989), page 23
9. Rick Renner, in *Sparkling Gems from the Greek: 365 New Gems to Equip and Empower You for Victory Every Day of the Year* (Tulsa, OK: Institute Books, 2016), pp. 436-437.
10. Rick Renner, in *Sparkling Gems from the Greek: 365 New Gems to Equip and Empower You for Victory Every Day of the Year* (Tulsa, OK: Institute Books, 2016), pp. 436-437.
11. Rick Renner, in *Sparkling Gems from the Greek: 365 New Gems to Equip and Empower You for Victory Every Day of the Year* (Tulsa, OK: Institute Books, 2016), pp. 436-437.

12. Chapter Twelve

1. *Rabbi Daniel Lapin (2012). "America's Real War", p.64, Multnomah*
2. Roberts Liardon, in *God's Generals: Why They Succeeded and Why Some Failed* (New Kensington, PA: Whitaker House, 2003), pp. 283-334.
3. esword Thayer's Greek Definitions
4. lecture notes, Dr. Ed Nelson
5. Mario Murillo, "Entitlement and Escapism," Mario Murillo Ministries, January 17, 2020, https://mariomurillo.org/2020/01/17/entitlement-and-escapism.

6. Rick Renner, in *Sparkling Gems from the Greek: 365 Greek Word Studies for Every Day of the Year to Sharpen Your Understanding of God's Word* (Tulsa, OK: Teach All Nations, 2003), pp. 536-537.
7. lecture notes, Dr. Benny Charles Hand
8. Kevin J. Conner, in *The Church in the New Testament* (Chichester, Eng.: Sovereign World, 1989), p. 80.
9. Alvin J. Schmidt, in *How Christianity Changed the World* (Grand Rapids , MI: Zondervan, 2004), pp. 25-27.
10. BibleAsk Team, "Were Hitler and Stalin's Governments Were Ordained to Be?," BibleAsk, December 12, 2020, https://bibleask.org/after-reading-romans-131-can-we-say-that-hitler-and-stalins-governments-were-ordained-to-be/.
11. Joseph Henry Thayer, Christian Gottlob Wilke, and Joseph Henry Thayer, *Greek-English Lexicon of the New Testament: Being Grimm's Wilke's Clavis Novi Testamenti* (Massachusetts: Hendrickson Pub., 1999).
12. Adele Berlin, Marc Zvi Brettler, and Michael Fishbane, *The Jewish Study Bible: Jewish Publication Society Tanakh Translation* (Oxford: Oxford University Press, 2004). page 28

www.ingramcontent.com/pod-product-compliance
Lightning Source LLC
Chambersburg PA
CBHW011147290426
44109CB00023B/2523